engage

C000040534

Prepare to be shocked. In
the scandalous stories of
surprising view of sex in Song of Songs; we'll watch Jesus
shaking the foundations of religion; and we'll tackle our
sickening sins with Paul. Get ready for some shocking stuff.

✱ DAILY READINGS Each day's
page throws you into the Bible, to
get you handling, questioning and
exploring God's message to you —
encouraging you to act on it and talk
to God more in prayer.

THIS ISSUE: Read some shocking
history in **1 Kings;** stamp on sin with
1 Corinthians; see God's view on sex
in **Song of Songs;** and walk in Jesus'
footsteps with **Matthew.**

✱ ESSENTIAL Articles on the
basics we really need to know about
God, the Bible and Christianity. This
issue, we look at what the Bible says
about **prayer.**

✱ TAKE IT FURTHER If you're
hungry for more at the end of an
engage page, turn to the **Take it
further** section to dig deeper.

✱ STUFF Articles on stuff relevant
to the lives of young Christians. This
issue: **What does the Bible say
about homosexuality?**

✱ REAL LIVES True stories,
revealing God at work in people's
lives. This time — **we smuggle
Bibles with Brother Andrew.**

✱ TOOLBOX is full of tools
to help you understand the Bible.
This issue we see how the Bible uses
repetition to teach us stuff.

✱ TRICKY tackles those mind-
bendingly tricky questions that
confuse us all, as well as questions
our friends bombard us with.
This time we ask: **Is Christianity
only for weak people?**

All of us who work on **engage** are
passionate to see the Bible at
work in people's lives. Do you
want God's word to have an
impact on your life? Then open
your Bible, and start on the first
engage study right now...

HOW TO USE engage

1 Set a time you can read the Bible every day

2 Find a place where you can be quiet and think

3 Grab your Bible, pen and a notebook

4 Ask God to help you understand what you read

5 Read the day's verses with engage, taking time to think about it

6 Pray about what you've read

BIBLE STUFF

We use the NIV Bible version, so you might find it's the best one to use with engage. If the notes say **"Read 1 Kings 1 v 1–14"**, look up 1 Kings in the contents page at the front of your Bible. It'll tell you which page 1 Kings starts on. Find chapter 1 of 1 Kings, and then verse 1 of chapter 1 (the verse numbers are the tiny ones). Then start reading. Simple.

In this issue...

THIS SHOCKING ISSUE OF ENGAGE IS BROUGHT TO YOU BY...

Scandalous scribes: Martin Cole   Cassie Martin   Carl Laferton   Helen Thorne

Disturbing designer: Steve Devane

Outrageous proof-readers: Anne Woodcock   Nicole Carter

Exaggerating editor: Martin Cole   (martin@thegoodbook.co.uk)

1 Kings

Ruling passion

If you think history is a snooze then 1 Kings is the book to wake you up. It's packed with power struggles, epic battles, heart-breaking drama and more twists and turns than a Hollywood thriller.

The action's set in the united kingdom of Israel, the nation God chose to be His very own. Then civil war breaks out and the kingdom splits in two — north (Israel) and south (Judah). The story is told through the two nations' kings. Some are good and some are bad. Some are really bad.

In 1 Kings, a good king submits to God and keeps His commands. He listens to God's spokesmen (prophets) and leads God people to do the same. He refuses to tolerate other gods.

David was a good king. God promised to make his son, Solomon, king after him. After a good start, Solomon turned bad. And after him, things got worse among God's people. Mostly their kings were terrible. God kept sending prophets to show He was still in charge and to tell people to turn back to Him.

As you read this royal blockbuster:
- observe God in the driving seat of history
- notice how powerful His words are
- watch God not afraid to judge His people
- see God keeping promises He made centuries earlier
- listen to God calling His people to love Him back
- and see how the shocking history of God's people under bad human kings points to the need for a perfect King from God.

If you're a Christian, you know this King personally. King Jesus. You won't find a better king than Him — not among all the rulers of God's people that you're about to meet...

3

1 | Son block

King David was old. And cold — he needed a human hot-water bottle. One of his sons, Adonijah, exploited his dad's old age to try to take over. But God wanted another of David's sons on the throne.

👁 Read 1 Kings 1 v 1–14

ENGAGE YOUR BRAIN
▷ Why was David's grip on power slipping? (v1–4)
▷ What did Adonijah do to exploit this? (v5, 7, 9)
▷ What did Nathan and Bathsheba do about it? (v11–14)

Bathsheba was one of David's wives and Solomon's mum. Nathan was God's spokesman — a prophet. They saw Adonijah's plot and decided to do something about it. Verses 15–27 go into the details.

👁 Read verses 28–40
▷ What did David do?
▷ How did he make sure Solomon was accepted by people as their new king? (v38–40)
▷ What was Benaiah's prayer? (v37)

At the start of the chapter, David seemed lifeless and useless but what a turnaround! David was decisive and made sure that Solomon would be king, with God's approval.

THINK IT OVER
▷ What gets you fired up and leaping into action?

👁 Read verses 41–53
▷ What did David recognise about God's involvement? (v47–48)
▷ How did Adonijah react? (v50)
▷ What was Adonijah's only chance of survival? (v52)

God had said Solomon would be king after David. God was in charge behind the scenes and He kept His word. As He always does.

PRAY ABOUT IT
Thank God that He's always in control. Ask Him to get you fired up and leaping into action over things that are important to Him.

→ TAKE IT FURTHER
For a little more, try page 108.

2 | Father's orders

Solomon is now king of Israel. His dad, David, is old and nearing death, but he still has some important words of advice for Solomon.

Read 1 Kings 2 v 1–4

ENGAGE YOUR BRAIN

◻ *What did David tell Solomon he must do? (v3)*

◻ *And what would be the results? v3: v4:*

David says that being a real man and having real strength means obeying God. If Solomon lived God's way He'd have success in everything he did.

Verse 4 is a massive one in 1 Kings. If Israel's kings stayed faithful to God and were careful to obey Him, then things would go well for them. Later, we'll find out the consequences of ignoring these wise words.

Read verses 5–12

◻ *What must Solomon do with Joab? (v6)*

◻ *Why? (v5)*

◻ *What about the guys in v7?*

◻ *What promise had David made to foul-mouthed Shimei? (v8)*

◻ *But what would Solomon do? (v9)*

Tomorrow we'll see if Solomon took his father's advice and showed strength as God's king.

GET ON WITH IT

◻ *Which of God's commands do you need to take more seriously?*
◻ *Whose advice should you listen to more?*
◻ *What changes do you need to make to walk in God's ways?*

PRAY ABOUT IT

Talk these things over with God right now.

THE BOTTOM LINE

Be strong and walk in God's ways.

→ **TAKE IT FURTHER**

Marching orders: go to page 108.

5

3 Enemy elimination

David had advised Solomon to kill Joab and Shimei for their crimes against God. Solomon also had to deal with his rebellious brother, Adonijah, who had promised to behave himself.

👁 Read 1 Kings 2 v 13–25

ENGAGE YOUR BRAIN

▶ *What did Adonijah ask for? (v17)*

▶ *Why did Solomon say no? (v22)*

▶ *What was the outcome? (v23–25)*

Adonijah sneakily used Solomon's mum in his devious plans to get Abishag, who had been one of King David's wives. Taking a previous king's wife was virtually claiming to be king yourself — Adonijah was trying to take Solomon's place as king. Solomon had warned Adonijah what would happen if he continued to be a bad lad and so he was killed.

👁 Read verses 26–35

▶ *Why did rebellious Abiathar escape the death sentence? (v26)*

▶ *Why was Joab killed? (v31–32)*

👁 Read verses 36–46

▶ *What deal did Solomon strike with Shimei? (v36–38)*

▶ *But what happened? (v39–40)*

▶ *For what two reasons was Shimei killed? (v42–44)*

These men had all disobeyed God and rebelled against God's chosen king. They paid for it with their lives. Solomon was now in a very strong position as king. When Jesus returns to establish His kingdom, He too will wipe out His enemies. You can't go against God and His King and survive.

PRAY ABOUT IT

Pray for people you know who openly speak against God and against King Jesus. Ask God to turn their lives upside down so they realise who's the boss and who they must worship.

→ TAKE IT FURTHER

To hear what Jesus said on this topic, turn to page 108.

4 Wise choice

King Solomon is now firmly in charge of God's people, Israel. But he's not most famous for his power. Solomon was well-known for his great wisdom — and here's how he got it.

👁 Read 1 Kings 3 v 1–3

ENGAGE YOUR BRAIN
▶ *What kind of king was Solomon? (v3)*

"High places" were worship centres away from Jerusalem where people made sacrifices to God. Later on, people started worshipping false gods at these places. But at this point they're OK-ish, but not ideal.

👁 Read verses 4–15
▶ *What was God's great offer? (v5)*

▶ *What was Solomon's surprising answer? (v9)*

▶ *What did God give him? (v12–14)*

▶ *Why? (v10–11)*

Solomon could have asked for any selfish thing — wealth, success, — but he asked for wisdom to serve God well. To those who long to live for God and serve Him, He gives them far more than they ask for or deserve.

👁 Read verses 16–28
▶ *How does this bizarre story show Solomon's great wisdom?*

▶ *What effect did it have on the people? (v28)*

God kept His word and gave King Sol great wisdom. Everyone was amazed at Solomon's wisdom and knew that it was from God. The Lord gives all His people different abilities to serve Him with. If we use them, people will see what a great God we serve.

PRAY ABOUT IT
What can you ask God for that would help you live for Him more? Thank God for His great faithfulness and generosity to His people.

→ TAKE IT FURTHER
More wise words on page 108.

5 | Let there be lists

Loads of lists today. There are two lists of important people. Then there's a shopping list of the huge amount Sol's household ate everyday. And finally we have a list of the great and wise things Solomon did. Dig in...

👁 Read 1 Kings 4 v 1–19

ENGAGE YOUR BRAIN

▷ *What are the two different lists? (v2, 7)*

What's the point of all these names? Well, they show us more of the wisdom that God gave Solomon. He made sure that Israel was ruled properly. Being wise sometimes means organising and planning things so they run smoothly. Admin may be boring but it can help us serve God more effectively.

👁 Read verses 20–28

▷ *How are God's people described? (v20)*

▷ *What did the nations around Israel do? (v21)*

▷ *What was life like for God's people during Sol's reign? (v24)*

God was keeping His promises to His people. They were now a huge, great nation, living in their own land in peace. If they continued to obey God, the future would be awesome.

👁 Read verses 29–34

▷ *How wise was Solomon? (v29–31)*

▷ *How did he use this wisdom? (v32–34)*

▷ *Where did it come from? (v29)*

Superb. God was reaching the world through Solomon. But Sol was far from perfect, as we'll see later on. God was being massively generous to a flawed human king.

PRAY ABOUT IT

Thank God that He gives us far more than we deserve. Thank Him for always keeping His promises. Thank Him for the best promise and best gift ever — sending Jesus to rescue us.

→ TAKE IT FURTHER

Feeling listless? Go to page 108.

6 | Grand designs

And now it's time for three chapters full of tiny details about building and furnishings. Hooray! If you're a fan of home-makeover TV, then you'll be excited. For the rest of us it seems a snooze. But there's important stuff here.

👁 **Read 1 Kings 5 v 1–12**

ENGAGE YOUR BRAIN

▶ What was Solomon's plan? (v5)

▶ Why could Solomon do what David couldn't? (v3–4)

▶ What was King Hiram's response? (v7, v10)

▶ What two things did God give Solomon? (v12)

Now let's pick out some of the details from chapters 5–7.

▶ Who built the temple? (v13–18)

▶ What did it look like? (6 v 14–18, 21–22, 29–30)

▶ What was the most important area? (6 v 19–20)

▶ How long did it take? (6 v 38)

▶ What else did Sol build? (7 v 1)

▶ How long did he spend on his own palace?

👁 **Read 1 Kings 6 v 11–13**

▶ What great promise did God make to Solomon?

In the middle of all the details about the temple and the palace, these verses show us what's important to God. He demands that His king and His people obey Him. The new temple was an impressive symbol of God living with His people, but He expected them to keep living for Him.

THINK IT OVER

▶ What things in your life stop you obeying God?

▶ How can you see God at work in your life?

PRAY ABOUT IT

Talk to God about your answers and ask Him to help you to live His way.

➜ **TAKE IT FURTHER**

More design tips on page 109.

7 ¦ Park the ark

Solomon (and thousands of workers) have finished building God's temple. So it's time for God to check out His new place.

👁 Read 1 Kings 8 v 1–9

ENGAGE YOUR BRAIN

▷ *What big event took place? (v1–2)*

▷ *Where did the priests park the ark? (v6)*

▷ *What was in the ark? (v9)*

The ark was a box which reminded God's people of His agreement (covenant) with them. It symbolised God's presence with them. If they obeyed God, they'd stay in the land.

👁 Read verses 10–13

▷ *What happened? (v10–11)*

▷ *What was Solomon's summary? (v12–13)*

The great God who is everywhere chose to share His presence with His people. He was near, yet He was far — there was no open access for an unholy people to a holy God. That would have to wait until Jesus came.

👁 Read verses 14–21

▷ *What promise did God keep? (v20)*

This was a great moment. God's temple was complete and His ark was now in the temple. God was with His people. Awesome. And He had kept His promises to King David. Everything was looking good for God's people. For now.

God always keeps His promises. The most incredible promise He made was to send His Son to rescue us. Jesus' death and resurrection have made it possible for us to have access to perfect, holy God.

PRAY ABOUT IT

You know what's on your heart today as you talk to God.

→ TAKE IT FURTHER

What are cherubim? Try page 109.

8 I'd like to thank...

It's speech time at Solomon's Building Awards Ceremony. But who will he thank? His mum? The 30,000 builders? Himself?

👁 **Read 1 Kings 8 v 22–30**

ENGAGE YOUR BRAIN

🔅 *Who's the only one that Sol thanks and praises? (v23)*

🔅 *What amazed Solomon? (v27)*

🔅 *What does he ask God for? (v30)*

Solomon could barely believe that huge, all-powerful God would live among His people. But knowing how great and loving God is led Sol to ask God to remember His people and forgive them.

🔅 *In what different circumstances?*
v31–32:
v33-34:
v35–36:
v37:
v41–43:
v44–45:
v46:

🔅 *What reason did Sol give for God forgiving His people? (v57–60)*

👁 **Read verses 54–66**

🔅 *What else did Sol ask God for? (v57–60)*

🔅 *What did God expect of Israel? (v61)*

🔅 *How did the Israelites thank God for all He'd done for them? (v62–66)*

God has a big plan for His people — "that all people of the earth may know that the Lord is God and that there is no other" (v60). He wants us to tell people about Him. But God doesn't just care about the big plan: He cares for our daily needs too (v59).

PRAY ABOUT IT

Bring your everyday needs and worries to God. And also pray about the "big" things — that people will turn to Jesus. Pray for specific people who need to turn to God.

➡ **TAKE IT FURTHER**

Heart of the matter on page 109.

11

9 | The golden age

King Solomon was at the height of his fame and Israel was experiencing a golden age. The second half of this chapter gives us the details. But before that, God spells out a word of warning.

👁 Read 1 Kings 9 v 1–9

ENGAGE YOUR BRAIN

▶ *How did God respond to yesterday's prayer? (v3)*

▶ *What did He tell Sol to do? (v4)*

▶ *What would be the result? (v5)*

▶ *But what was the warning? (v9)*

We shouldn't take God's warnings negatively. God shows great love and kindness in reminding us what we need to do to please Him and the consequences if we don't.

👁 Skim read verses 10–28

This section provides a snapshot of life in Israel during Solomon's reign. We get political details (v10–14) including King Hiram sending David 4 tons of gold for his building projects! We get a glimpse of the huge number of people involved in all this work (v15–24). Solomon continued to worship God and offer the right sacrifices (v25). He also had an impressive navy and sea trade (v26–28).

Everything was going well for God's king and God's people. But it's often when life's going well that the devil attacks and we mess up big time. Solomon needed to listen to God's warning in v4–9. And so do we. Sometimes we can cruise through life enjoying it so much that we fail to notice we're no longer obeying God so much. Or He's slipped way down our priorities.

PRAY ABOUT IT

Ask God to give you integrity of heart and a real desire to serve and obey Him. Thank Him that because of Jesus, believers now have the Holy Spirit to help them live for God.

THE BOTTOM LINE

Obey God or else.

→ TAKE IT FURTHER

No *Take it further* section today.

Royal visit

God had given Solomon such great wisdom and impressive wealth that word soon got around. The queen of Sheba had heard about Solomon and his God and was curious to discover whether the rumours were true.

👁 **Read 1 Kings 10 v 1–13**

ENGAGE YOUR BRAIN

▶ *Why did this queen visit Solomon? (v1–2)*

▶ *What impressed her? (v3–5)*

▶ *What did she realise about Sol's success? (v9)*

The queen of Sheba was bowled over by Solomon's wisdom and his impressive kingdom. And she saw where it came from — God had made Solomon king and given him all his wisdom and wealth. In return, God expected Sol to rule with justice and righteousness — pleasing God.

👁 **Read verses 14–29**

▶ *What did Solomon do with all the gold he received? (v16–21)*

▶ *How is Sol's wisdom and wealth described? (v23–24)*

▶ *Who was behind it all?*

The writer of 1 Kings gives us a tour of Solomon's treasuries — it's an impressive sight. God had kept His promise to give Solomon wealth and wisdom. God's kingdom was in great shape. But it wouldn't last — Solomon and the Israelites would turn away from God and life would never be as good again.

Yet one day there will be an even greater kingdom. Jesus will return to gather all believers to live in the perfect kingdom with Him.

PRAY ABOUT IT

Thank God for His gift of wisdom. Ask Him to give you a greater insight into what He's like and what He expects of you. And get ready for eternal life with the only perfect King — King Jesus.

→ **TAKE IT FURTHER**

More royal info on page 109.

11 | Fatal attraction

Solomon had become the greatest king in the world. He had immense wisdom, gold and fame. And he was given spices, ivory, weapons. And baboons. But would he use all this to serve God alone?

👁 Read 1 Kings 11 v 1–13

ENGAGE YOUR BRAIN

- ▶ *What did Solomon do wrong?*
- ▶ *Why was this so bad? (v3–6)*
- ▶ *What would God do? (v11)*
- ▶ *What kindness did God show? (v12–13)*

👁 Read verses 14–25

- ▶ *Why did Hadad want revenge against Israel? (v14–17)*
- ▶ *Who else caused trouble for Solomon? (v23–25)*
- ▶ *Why? (v23, 11)*

👁 Read verses 26–43

- ▶ *What did the prophet Ahijah predict about Jeroboam? (v31)*
- ▶ *What promise did God make to Jeroboam? (v37–38)*
- ▶ *How did God keep His promises to David? (v34–36)*
- ▶ *What was the next big event in Israel's history? (v43)*

Solomon disobeyed God, had many foreign wives and allowed them to turn him against God. For this disgusting idol worship, Israel would be split in two and Sol's family would now rule only one tribe (Judah) instead of all twelve. Yet God had promised David that his family would continue to rule God's people. Despite Solomon's sin, God would keep His promise. There was still hope David's family and God's people (v39). This hope would be finally and fully realised when God sent Jesus.

GET ON WITH IT

- ▶ *What do you worship instead of God?*
- ▶ *Who might lead you away from the Lord?*
- ▶ *What do you need to do about it?*

PRAY ABOUT IT

Talk to God about these things, asking Him to keep you close to Him. Thank Him for the certain hope brought by Jesus.

➔ TAKE IT FURTHER

More stuff on page 109.

12 The big split

Solomon turned away from God and so the Lord said He would take most of Israel away from Solomon and his family. Sol's son, Rehoboam, was now king, but he definitely wasn't wise like his dad...

👁 Read 1 Kings 12 v 1–15

ENGAGE YOUR BRAIN
- ▶ *What did the people want from their new king? (v4)*

- ▶ *What did the elders advise? (v7)*

- ▶ *But what did Rehoboam do? (v13–14)*

- ▶ *Why did all this happen? (v15)*

After Solomon's death, rival Jeroboam was back in town. And he led the Israelites to Rehoboam, the new king. They demanded less forced labour, less taxes and less army service. Rehoboam took advice. From the wrong people. Big mistake. Yet this was all part of God's plan (v15).

👁 Read verses 16–24
- ▶ *What did most of Israel do? (v16, 20)*

- ▶ *Who stayed loyal to David's family and Rehoboam?*

- ▶ *What did Rehob plan next? (v21)*

- ▶ *What stopped him? (v24)*

The Israelites told Rehoboam to take a hike and the kingdom split in two. Finally Rehoboam stopped making terrible decisions and listened to God. The Lord stepped in to stop the king making even worse mistakes. God was still looking out for His people.

We all make mistakes and sin against God. Yet He still loves us and wants us to turn back to Him. He usually makes it clear when we're displeasing Him and calls us back. It's up to us whether or not we listen to Him.

GET ON WITH IT
- ▶ *What do you need to stop doing?*

- ▶ *Which of God's warnings do you need to listen to more?*

→ TAKE IT FURTHER
Split up and go to page 110.

Homosexuality

There seem to be so many different "Christian" views on homosexuality. At one extreme, you have the placard-waving mob telling us that "God hates gays". At the other, you have the openly gay bishops who declare it's totally fine for Christians to be in a loving, gay relationship because God is a God of love. But what does the Bible say?

SEX IS GOOD

Firstly, what does the Bible say about sex? Well, it's good! God created it before the fall — before humanity rejected His rule — and so it was a good God-given gift (Genesis 2 v 24). It was also designed to be something special: a way of bonding together one man and one woman in marriage. Jesus quotes this part of Genesis in Mark 10 v 6–9 and makes the same point. So sex is not designed to be enjoyed outside marriage, and it is heterosexual marriage at that.

IGNORING GOD

Anything less than that is not how God wants things to be. Sadly, as we know, Genesis 3 follows Genesis 2 and humanity starts disobeying and rejecting God's rules. If you disregard the maker's instructions, you're going to make a mess of things — putting a metal spoon in your microwave is never a good idea, as the instructions clearly state!

God makes it very clear to His people, Israel, in the Old Testament, that ignoring His blueprint for sex is not just foolish but dangerous. Whether it be adultery, sex outside marriage or homosexuality, God is not pleased when we disregard His plan (see Leviticus chapter 18).

Fast-forward several hundred years and the non-Jewish world was disregarding and disobeying God just as much. Check out Romans 1 v 18–32. The wrong attitude to and use of sex is just one example of how humanity has rejected God, provoking His totally justified anger. Homosexual sex (both gay and lesbian) is listed there with other examples of how we've decided we want to use God's gifts and set the rules rather than Him. Just as Adam and Eve did.

DOES GOD HATE GAY PEOPLE?

No, God does not hate gay people. In fact, He loves them so much that He sent His one and only Son to die for them. Often, Christians treat homosexuality as the worst, unforgivable sin. But we are all sinners and nobody's sexuality is as perfect as God created and intended it to be. A lustful glance or impure thoughts are far from God's ideal, no matter which sex they are focused on. We are all sexual sinners.

BRAND NEW

"If anyone is in Christ, they are a new creation; the old has gone, the new has come!" (2 Corinthians 5 v 17). Jesus' death and resurrection cleanse us from all our sins and give us new life. We're forgiven and perfect in God's sight. Look at 1 Corinthians 6 v 9–11. Many different sins are listed including homosexual sex; *"And that is what some of you were. But you were washed, you were sanctified, you were justified in the name of the Lord Jesus Christ and by the Spirit of our God"* (v11).

TOUGH LOVE

The Bible tells us that this is not the way God wants His people to live. That is tough. If you have homosexual longings, then it's very hard to know that if you want to live God's way, you can't express them. Maybe it means you'll never marry or enter into a civil partnership with someone you love. But the Christian life is not easy. There are many things we have to say no to when we say yes to God.

But as Jesus tells His followers in Matthew 10 v 38–39: *"Anyone who does not take his cross and follow me is not worthy of me. Whoever finds his life will lose it, and whoever loses his life for my sake will find it."* Struggles and sufferings in this life are cancelled out by the glorious future Jesus promises His friends and by the wonderful gift of His presence with us now.

There is so much more that could be said, but if you or a friend is struggling with same-sex attraction, then there are Christian organisations that can help. Make sure they are seeking to obey what God says on the issue and that they are not promising more than the Bible does. A good place to start in the UK is: http://truefreedomtrust.co.uk

1 Corinthians

God, the bad & the ugly

Paul's writing to the church in Corinth, Greece. The city was a bit of a first-century Los Angeles — people from many cultures and religions at an international crossroads. And you name it, it was happening there.

It had a new church, started by Paul a few years earlier (see Acts 18 v 1–9), but it was having big problems. You thought your church was struggling? Well, this church managed to be lively, divided, exuberant, arrogant, immoral and confused all at once. It was in real danger of destroying itself. Still, they wrote to Paul for help and 1 Corinthians is his reply, written in the early 50s AD.

In the first half of the letter, he deals with what he's heard about them. Then he answers their questions. He starts the letter by pointing them back: reminding them of Jesus' death on the cross and how that affects them. He ends by pointing them forward: to Jesus' return, and the

prospect of being transformed to be like Him.

So the letter is good for us too, since we're also living between those two events. And it tackles controversial subjects like sex outside of marriage, spiritual gifts and Christian leaders who deny the resurrection. It's all here!

But Paul's burning aim here is to urge these Christians to think of others. To stop being proudly independent and to start thinking and behaving in ways which put others first, whoever those people might be. I think we all need to hear that message.

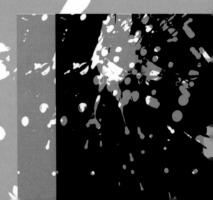

13 | Introducing...

It's time for some introductions. Let's meet and greet Paul, the church in Corinth and, er, Sosthenes. No, we're not sure who he is either. And the biggest introduction of all is given to God Himself.

Read 1 Corinthians 1 v 1–3

ENGAGE YOUR BRAIN

How does Paul introduce himself?

How does he describe the church in Corinth?

Who else is the letter for? (v2)

This whole, long letter is a big challenge to a church who had all kinds of problems. Paul's hello is a challenge too. He says they've been "sanctified" (made holy) — so they've got to live like that in practice. Because they're "called to be holy".

Read verses 4–9

What positive things does Paul say about this church?
v4:
v5:
v6:
v7:

What will be true in the future? (v8)

Why? (v9)

This church may have serious problems, but Paul thinks of it first from God's point of view. It's God's church, not Paul's, so Paul reminds them about Him. God, that is.

PRAY ABOUT IT

These things are true for all Christians. Spend time thanking God for them now:
• We've received God's grace through Jesus.
• Jesus enriches and improves what we know and what we say.
• We don't lack spiritual gifts — God has given us so many abilities to use for Him.
• He will keep us strong.
• One day He will make us perfect and sinless.
• God has called us and is totally faithful.

→ TAKE IT FURTHER

Introducing more facts on page 110.

19

14 Long division

Divided, arrogant, tolerating dreadful behaviour and unbiblical thinking: Corinth makes even your church look great. But Paul's excellent advice for them can teach us loads too.

👁 Read 1 Corinthians 1 v 10–12

ENGAGE YOUR BRAIN

▶ What did Paul want for this church? (v10)

▶ What were they arguing about? (v12)

Divisions in churches are nothing new, and cliques form fast around powerful leaders — even those leaders who don't want them. As we'll see, the Corinthians were easily dazzled by claims for great success.

👁 Read verses 13–17

▶ What are the answers to the questions in v13?

▶ What was Paul sent to do? (v17)

▶ So why should they worship Jesus and not Paul or any other leader?

Christians argue about lots of different issues. Sometimes followers of different leaders or different types of churches argue. But it's pointless. Our focus should not be on the small things. And we certainly shouldn't hero-worship our leaders. The focus must always be Christ and His death and resurrection. Whatever we disagree about seems pathetic in comparison to that. So Christians can put aside their differences and be united by Jesus and what He's done.

THINK IT OVER

▶ Who do you argue with about Christian stuff?

▶ Are you ever guilty of hero worship?

▶ What do you need to do about these things?

→ TAKE IT FURTHER

Divide and conquer on page 110.

15 | Foolish wisdom

The message of Jesus doesn't always go down well. In fact, people often ridicule it and hate it. But that doesn't mean it's not true and vital. Paul explains...

👁 Read 1 Corinthians 1 v 18–25

ENGAGE YOUR BRAIN
- ▶ *How is the gospel viewed by different people? (v18)*
- ▶ *Why does the message of the cross seem foolish?*
- ▶ *But why is it so effective? (v18, 21)*

Many Jews wanted a military hero to zap the Romans, and the Greeks wanted a clever argument to persuade them. But the message of Jesus is that He died on the cross to save people — and that just seems crazy to so many people. They don't see the power of God behind it.

👁 Read verses 26–31
- ▶ *What's the great news for those of us who feel useless? (v26–28)*
- ▶ *What has Jesus done for believers? (v30)*
- ▶ *So how should that affect their attitude? (v29, 31)*

God saves His people this way because it gives Him more glory. It's all down to God, not us. The gospel shows how amazing God is.

👁 Read 1 Corinthians 2 v 1–5
- ▶ *How does Paul describe the way he shared the gospel with them? (v1–4)*
- ▶ *Why did he do this? (v5)*

God hasn't chosen you because you're clever or successful or gorgeous or holy. What a relief! If we trust in Jesus, God accepts us despite all our failings. And He can use us in great ways. But we need to expect a negative response to the gospel much of the time while remembering God's wisdom and power behind it.

PRAY ABOUT IT
Talk to God about everything that's on your mind and heart today.

→ TAKE IT FURTHER
Big questions on page 110.

21

16 Spirit of wisdom

Many people think the message of the cross is foolish. But Paul says it is wise. Not human wisdom, but God's wisdom. Get ready for more mind-blowing truths...

👁 Read 1 Corinthians 2 v 6–10

ENGAGE YOUR BRAIN

▷ How long has God had His perfect plan? (v7)

▷ What does the plan involve that confused so many people? (v8)

▷ How has God made this secret plan known? (v10)

The cross: planned before time and effective into eternity. It couldn't be understood by sight, hearing or thought (v9). God chose to reveal His plan by sending Jesus. And He helps us understand the cross by the Holy Spirit. Brilliant.

👁 Read verse 10–16

▷ What has every Christian received? (v12)

▷ And what will the Spirit help us do? (v12)

Verses 14–16 are tricky. "The man without the Spirit" means non-Christians. To them, talk of God's plan and the cross just seems stupid. They can't understand it.

The "spiritual man" probably means a more mature Christian. He can "judge all things" because he works out how they link in with God's great plan, the cross of Jesus — and he's not swayed by any human "wisdom" (v15).

God is the source of all wisdom (v16) — no one advises Him. He's revealed His plan, giving us "the mind of Christ". We're becoming more like Jesus. How amazing is that?

PRAY ABOUT IT

Thank God for His great plan and what it teaches us about Him — the God who is Father, Son and Spirit. One God, three persons.

→ **TAKE IT FURTHER**

More wise words on page 111.

17 | Building blocked

The Corinthians may have become Christians, but they didn't act like it. In fact, they were totally immature. They were big kids who needed to grow up into mature Christians.

👁 **Read 1 Corinthians 3 v 1–9**

ENGAGE YOUR BRAIN

▶ *Why weren't these guys as spiritual as they thought they were? (v3)*

▶ *What did they argue about? (v4)*

▶ *But how should we view Christian leaders? (v5–7)*

👁 **Read verse 9–17**

▶ *How does Paul describe the church? (v9)*

▶ *What was Paul's job? (v10)*

▶ *What should be the foundation of a church? (v11)*

Paul says it's possible to build on the right foundations (Jesus) but with the wrong building materials — like stupid arguments and arrogance in the church at Corinth. They were in danger of destroying the church, not building it up (v17).

Christians can be sure of eternal life. But they must also ensure the work they do for God is top quality and based on Jesus. The church is God's temple. He lives with His people (v16). So foolish leaders, who go about destroying His church, can expect trouble (v17).

👁 **Read verse 18–23**

▶ *How do these verses sum up the first three chapters?*

We need to realise that everything comes from God, so we shouldn't hero-worship and we souldn't boast about ourselves. It's all down to God.

PRAY ABOUT IT

Thank God that, in Christ, all things are yours! He gives us everything we need. Ask Him to help you live in a way that shows this and doesn't cause division with other Christians.

➡ **TAKE IT FURTHER**

Build up to page 111.

18 | Scum of the earth

This church had big problems — hero worship, big arguments and arrogance among others. Well, Paul was not the type to keep quiet. Get ready for some straight talking.

👁 Read 1 Corinthians 4 v 1–7

ENGAGE YOUR BRAIN

- ▷ *What's the job of Christian leaders? (v1–2)*
- ▷ *Whose job is it to judge and how will He do it? (v3–5)*
- ▷ *What must these guys remember? (v6–7)*

We must not treat Christian leaders as perfect people. Or be too critical of them. It's Jesus' job to judge them (v5). And we shouldn't think too highly of ourselves. Everything we have has been given to us (v7).

👁 Read verses 8–13

- ▷ *How did the Corinthians view themselves? (v8, 10)*
- ▷ *What was life like for Paul and the other gospel-spreaders?*

Paul was being sarcastic. This church thought they were great and had everything they needed, but they were trusting in the wrong things. Life for Christians isn't easy — serving God can lead to ridicule, dishonour, poverty, bullying and being treated like the scum of the earth.

👁 Read verses 14–21

- ▷ *How does Paul show his care for them? (v14–17)*
- ▷ *What should they do? (v16)*
- ▷ *What will Paul do? (v18–21)*

THINK IT OVER

- ▷ *What do you expect the Christian life to be like?*
- ▷ *What should you expect it to be like? Why?*
- ▷ *Are you willing to be treated in the same way as Jesus?*

PRAY ABOUT IT

Pray that you'll become more like Paul, who became more like Christ.

THE BOTTOM LINE

The Christian life is hard but so incredibly rewarding.

→ TAKE IT FURTHER

Even more on page 111.

Use your loaf

Sex. Sex. Sex. Corinth was obsessed with it. Paul heard that not only was the church infected by sexual disobedience, but it tolerated it. So Paul waded in.

👁 Read 1 Corinthians 5 v 1–8

ENGAGE YOUR BRAIN

- ▶ *What was the problem? (v1)*
- ▶ *What was the church's response?*
- ▶ *What do you think v5 means? (also see v2)*
- ▶ *What does the church need to do and why? (v6–8)*

The church accepted this hideous behaviour! Paul was furious. His wise plan (v5) was that the discipline would destroy the man's sinful nature, but the man himself would be saved. So the church should kick him out, handing him over to Satan's sphere of influence — the world. He must be shown that what he's doing is wrong.

Verses 6–8 are a lesson in purity. A special loaf was baked to celebrate Passover. Its ingredients had to be kept separate from other bread. Paul said that because we celebrate a special Passover (Jesus' death), our lives should be as fresh and different as that new loaf. So throw out sin.

👁 Read verses 9–13

- ▶ *Who should they not associate with in the church? (v11)*
- ▶ *Does that mean staying away from all sinful people? (v10)*

Paul is saying that we should let God judge the world, but we should keep His standards in the church. And this isn't something any one of us can do on our own as we're all sinful, so the whole church should be seen to act.

THINK IT OVER

- ▶ *Give yourself a mark out of ten for your behaviour with: a) sex b) money c) possessions d) drink*
- ▶ *What do you need to change?*
- ▶ *Do you tend to judge sin outside the church but tolerate it with your Christian friends?*

Talk to God about these things and ask His help to get the balance right.

→ TAKE IT FURTHER

More sex advice on page 111.

20 | Court order

Disaster. Some of these arrogant Corinthian Christians were suing each other in court. Stunned, Paul appeals to them not to behave as everyone else in the world does.

👁 Read 1 Corinthians 6 v 1–7

ENGAGE YOUR BRAIN

▶ What should Christians in big disagreements with each other do? (v2, 4–5)

▶ Why? (v3)

▶ Why is Christian vs Christian in court so bad? (v6–7)

Verse 3 is out of this world — Christians have a future role to play in God's final judgment (more in *Take it further*). So what we see and do now is far less important than what we'll see and do in the future. Churches should deal with disputes themselves so they're not a bad witness to non-Christians.

👁 Read verses 8–11

People who continue this way (see the list in v9–10) will only have God's punishment to look forward to. That's true for all the "wicked" — those who refuse Jesus' rescue. Christians need to remember they've been changed (v11).

THINK IT OVER

▶ What has Jesus done for us? (v11)

▶ Describe in your own words how that changes us.

▶ What do you need to ask God to help you with right now?

PRAY ABOUT IT

Some of us have sordid pasts. God forgives everything believers have done and makes it possible for them to change — from the inside. Stop to thank God for the changes in your character and behaviour since you became a Christian.

▶ What do you need to ask God to help you with right now?

→ TAKE IT FURTHER

Follow orders and go to page 111.

God's body

Some people thought: God guarantees our forgiveness, so it's OK to do what we like. God's only interested in our spiritual lives. So there's nothing wrong with sex outside of marriage and stuff like that.

👁 **Read 1 Corinthians 6 v 12–17**

ENGAGE YOUR BRAIN

▶ What is Paul's double answer to their view? (v12)

▶ How important are our bodies to God? (v13–14)

▶ Why does it matter what we do with our bodies? (v15–17)

These Christians said they had freedom and could do whatever they wanted. But freedom isn't the only issue — what's good for you and who controls you also matter (v13). Your body is owned by God. He wants to rule what you do with it. You'll have your body for eternity when he raises you from the dead — as He raised Jesus (v14).

Christian are actually joined with Christ. So how can a member of Christ's body become one with a prostitute by sex? The idea's appalling. And it's true for any sex outside marriage, even when the two are "in love".

👁 **Read verses 18–20**

▶ What's the only safe option when tempted? (start of v18)

▶ Why else should we keep our bodies pure?
v19:
v20:

PRAY ABOUT IT

You might have specific sins to confess today. Ask for God's deep forgiveness and His power to run away from sin. And work out one way to obey the positive command at the end of v20.

THE BOTTOM LINE

Christians are united with Christ so should keep their bodies pure.

→ **TAKE IT FURTHER**

Body of evidence on page 111.

22 | God, sex and marriage

The Christians in Corinth had problems with sex and relationships, so Paul gave them loads of practical advice on sex, marriage and staying single. Part one today, with more over the next two days.

👁 Read 1 Corinthians 7 v 1–9

▶ *What do you think some of the Corinthians had claimed? (v1)*

▶ *But what did Paul suggest? (v2, v3–5)*

▶ *What does he say about staying single? (v7–9)*

Paul isn't saying that everyone should get married, but that married people should only sleep with their partners. And in v9, Paul's saying that if someone has failed to control their sexual desires, then they should get married. Here, "burning with passion" doesn't mean bursting with sexual energy, but feeling pain and guilt about it.

👁 Read verses 10–16

If a marriage is hard-going, divorce isn't an option. Only separation is. Then there's the choice of remaining unmarried or being reconciled with your husband/wife (v11).

If there are two non-Christians and one becomes a believer, some people thought they should leave the non-Christian. But Paul says stick at it if the other partner is willing to (v12–14). But if the unbeliever insists on leaving, then it's OK to get divorced.

THINK IT OVER

▶ *Some people think they're only fulfilled if they're married. What would Paul say to them?*

▶ *Some think they're only fulfilled if they're sexually active. What would Paul say to them?*

▶ *How has this study changed your view of sex and marriage?*

▶ *Is there any action you need to take or stuff to pray over?*

→ TAKE IT FURTHER

More sex tips on page 112.

23 | Single minded

Do you agree with these statements? If sex is only for marriage, that makes marriage highly desirable. You don't have to be married to be a good Christian. In a sex-mad society we could become marriage-mad Christians.

👁 **Read 1 Corinthians 7 v 17–24**

ENGAGE YOUR BRAIN

▶ What's Paul's big rule? (v17)

▶ How do you think this applies to marriage and relationships?

▶ What's more important to God? (v19)

If you're a Christian, it doesn't matter whether you're a slave or free, or if you're married or not. It's not that important. Change won't make you a better Christian. We shouldn't get hung up on marriage or relationships or let it get in the way of us obeying God with our lives.

👁 **Read verses 25–31**

▶ What did Paul say to people who wondered whether they should marry? (v25–26)

▶ So is it wrong to marry? (v28)

▶ What's the warning? (v28)

▶ What should be our attitude to our time on earth? (v29–31)

▶ Why? (v31)

Jesus said there's no marriage in heaven — so if people are married today, they won't be then. Marriage is a phase — a good phase — that some people go through. But our relationship with Jesus is the one that lasts into eternity.

PRAY ABOUT IT

Take extra time to talk your situation through with God and pray for a friend (married/single/inbetween) who's finding life hard. Some people get anxious about who or whether they'll marry. Ask God to give them (or yourself) the right attitude.

THE BOTTOM LINE

Keeping God's commands is what really counts.

➔ **TAKE IT FURTHER**

Marriage guidance on page 112.

24 | Marriage proposal

More sex talk. What are the benefits of staying single? Why is marriage hard? How far can we go, sex-wise, before we're married?

👁 Read 1 Corinthians 7 v 32–35

ENGAGE YOUR BRAIN

▷ What's a major benefit of being a single Christian? (v32, 34)

▷ How can marriage distract Christians from serving God? (v33–34)

▷ What should all Christians aim for? (v35)

Sure, you gain a lot in marriage: a friend, helper, and sex too. But none of those necessarily helps us to know Jesus better. And marriage might distract us from serving Him fully.

👁 Read verses 36–40

▷ What's the advice for the man who won't get round to marrying his fiancee? (v36)

▷ What about "just good friends" who worry they might get left on the shelf? (v37–38)

▷ What's the advice for widows? (v39–40)

▷ Who should Christians date? (v39)

Paul says: if you're not ready for marriage, then you're not ready for sex. And that includes anything that might lead you on the road to sex. Play it safe. Remember, there are far more important things than sex and marriage (v19). That's why it's sometimes better to stay single and focus on being devoted to God (v40).

GET ON WITH IT

▷ How can you serve Jesus with "undivided devotion"?

▷ Anxious to get married? What would Paul say to you?

▷ How do you need to approach your relationship (or your attitude to sex) differently?

▷ What action will you take?

→ TAKE IT FURTHER

Even more on page 112.

25 Food fight

Another issue split the church — the sacrifice of food on pagan altars. It was a big deal back then. You wouldn't just throw a burger on the BBQ, you'd offer it to a god first. Most food sold in shops was offered to a god too.

Some Christians had no problems with such food. They knew there was only one God and that other gods didn't exist. But other Christians were worried — isn't eating that food like idol worship? They couldn't do it.

Read 1 Corinthians 8 v 1–6

ENGAGE YOUR BRAIN

- *What was the real problem here? (v1–2)*
- *What does Paul remind them about idols? (v4)*
- *And about God? (v6)*

The real problem wasn't food but their attitude. Some people in the church were know-it-alls. They chased after great knowledge. But it's more important to love God and be known by Him (v3). As for eating idols' food, these guys must remember that the Lord is the only God.

Read verses 7–13

- *What was the problem with some people? (v7)*

- *So what should a "stronger" Christian's attitude be? (v9, 13)*
- *Why? (v10–12)*

Christ has set us free, so we're free to eat what we like. The problem here was that weaker Christians felt guilty that they might have been worshipping idols. In that case, stronger Christians should stay away from idol food so that they're not a bad influence on others.

Yes, we have freedom. But what we do and say has an impact on other Christians. We have a responsibility for their spiritual growth. These days, the issue might be sex, alcohol, what you watch or anything that might be a stumbling block for others.

PRAY ABOUT IT

Ask God to help you be a good influence on other Christians, making wise decisions in the way you live.

→ TAKE IT FURTHER

Nibble a little more on page 112.

31

Prayer

In *Essential*, we take time out to explore key truths about God, the Bible and Christianity. This issue we ask: what is prayer and why should we pray?

God is huge. He is perfect, holy and powerful. He's in charge of the universe and knows everything that goes on. But He's not stuck in heaven running things from afar. He is involved in His world. He invites people to join His family by trusting in Jesus. And He takes pleasure in being intimately involved in our lives and communicating with us. Prayer is part of that communication.

YOU CAN TALK!

At its heart, prayer is talking to God. Because of Jesus, all Christians have access to their heavenly Father (1 Timothy 2 v 5). If we tried to call the Queen of England or the President of America we probably wouldn't get through. But we have the guaranteed privilege of being able to speak to someone even more powerful whenever we want.

That's exciting news! But being able to speak to God isn't just a great opportunity; it's an essential part of our Christian lives.

TALK THE TALK TO WALK THE WALK

You see, prayer is not about mindlessly chatting or selfishly asking for what we want. God isn't some kind of cosmic wish-granter who is programmed to provide us with a new girlfriend, phone or car on demand. And it's not about telling God what we need — He knows that already (Matt 6 v 7–8)! It's about growing in our relationship with God and getting involved in His work.

So how should we pray? By talking to God about the things He is passionate about. And by asking for things that are consistent with His character (that's doing what the Bible calls *"praying in Jesus' name"* — John 14 v 13–14).

We can:
- thank God for who He is and the great things He has done;
- say sorry for the times we haven't lived His way;
- ask for His guidance and for Him to provide for our needs;
- pray that more people will start following Jesus and get to know Him better;
- ask for God to help leaders rule wisely;
- ask Him to heal the sick.

And it's good to keep talking to Him about these things (Luke 18 v 1–8). If you find it hard to remember what to pray about, the prayer Jesus taught His disciples is a fantastic summary (Luke 11 v 1–4). And you can be sure that the Holy Spirit will help you too (Romans 8 v 26–27).

IT'S GOOD TO TALK

When we pray, we do some exciting things. We put our faith into action. We show that we are trusting and relying on God, believing in His promises and His power to act. We show that we care about His kingdom. And all these things help to deepen our relationship with God — as well as making a difference in the world.

TALKING TO A BRICK WALL?

But does God actually answer prayer? The Bible says yes (Luke 11 v 13). Whether we pray on our own (Matthew 6 v 6) or with others (Matthew 18 v 19–20), God will always hear His children. His understanding of the world is way better than ours and so He doesn't always give us the answer we expect. But He can be trusted to do what's right. His answers will sometimes make us happy, and always help us to become more holy.

TALK, TALK

So why not pray right now? You don't need to close your eyes or go somewhere special. You don't need to use set words or put on a different voice. Simply spend some time remembering how great God is and then talk to Him about the things that matter to you both, confident that He is willing and able to act.

Song of Songs

God, sex and wow

It's time to seek out one of the most avoided books in the Bible. It tackles the themes of love, sex and marriage in surprising detail. It's not for the squeamish and it's very mushy too. No wonder it rarely gets mentioned in church!

Remember wise King Solomon from 1 Kings? Well, he's behind this book. Actually, it's a poem or love song — a passionate celebration of God-given sexual love within the context of marriage.

There are two main characters: a woman (referred to in most Bible versions as "beloved") and a shepherd (the "lover"). And there's a group of the woman's friends who chip in. We overhear the man and woman talking, but we're also let in on their dreams, doubts and desires.

These characters talk a lot about love. They express the fact that it's one of God's great gifts. And they talk of its beauty and how sex is exclusive (and kept within marriage). Love and sex are precious so we shouldn't misuse them. God intends that such intense love is a normal part of marital life.

But this isn't just a mushy love poem. As we saw in 1 Corinthians, marriage is also a picture of our intimate relationship with Christ. So we'll also learn more about God, His love for us and our devotion to Him.

Are you ready to go where many Christians fear to tread — looking into the Song of Songs in detail? Remember to leave your dirty thoughts at the door and join us for an explanation of true love.

26 ¦ Snog of snogs

Are you ready for the song to beat all songs? It's a love song, so prepare yourself for lots of mushiness, staring into each other's eyes and comparing each other to fluffy animals.

Read Song of Songs 1 v 1–8

ENGAGE YOUR BRAIN

- *What does this lovestruck girl long for? (v2, 4)*
- *How does she describe herself? (v5–6)*

There's no doubt she's fallen head over heels for this guy. She describes him as her king and longs to be swept off her feet by him (v4). By the way, we'll assume that any sex or naughty stuff would be saved for marriage, as that's what the Bible always teaches.

Read 1 v 9 – 2 v 2

- *How would you describe their relationship?*
- *What are modern equivalents of their compliments?*

It's their way of saying to each other: "You're the best!" She thinks she's a plain, ordinary flower, but he says she makes everyone else seem like ugly thorns (2 v 1–2).

THINK IT OVER

What do you look for in a partner? An awesome body? Or something else? We've no reason to think that the woman's a supermodel and the man's Mr Perfect. But that's how they describe each other.

- *What's the lesson here for us?*

Read verses 3–7

- *How's she feeling now? (v3–6)*
- *What's her warning? (v7)*

Verses 4–5 might mean he wants to make love to her and she can't wait for the day (when they're married, of course). But she warns her friends not to ignite sexual feelings until the time is right (v7). More on this later.

PRAY ABOUT IT

Ask God to teach you the truth about love through the Song of Songs. Thank Him that love like this is stamped with His approval.

→ TAKE IT FURTHER

Low self-esteem? Turn to page 113.

27 Long of longings

Intoxicating stuff, this Song of Songs. It's not surprising — a love like this is all-absorbing, it's overpowering, it's everything.

👁 Read Song of Songs 2 v 8–17

ENGAGE YOUR BRAIN

🔘 What's got her heart thumping? (v8–9)

🔘 What's exciting about his invitation? (v10–13)

🔘 What feelings does he express? (v14)

🔘 What is she particularly excited about? (v16)

Song of Songs is ancient Eastern poetry so a lot of its images sound weird to us (eg: a man as a gazelle, v9). But it's obvious how they view each other, and that love is bursting into life, like flowers in springtime (v11–13).

👁 Read Song of Songs 3 v 1–5

🔘 What's the crisis? (v1)

🔘 How does she repeatedly refer to him in these verses?

🔘 What made her happy? (v4)

🔘 Why do you think yesterday's warning is repeated here? (v5)

Being in love can send you crazy with worry and desire. But we've got to be very careful not to let it take over from what's most important (serving God). And make sure we don't awaken love and sexual desire when we're not ready for it.

PRAY ABOUT IT

Pray for Christians you know who are in love (maybe yourself). Pray that their love will be pleasing to God and that they're not tempted into sex outside of marriage.

THE BOTTOM LINE

Love can be overwhelming.

→ TAKE IT FURTHER

More top tips on page 113.

28 Song of sex

What do you think of weddings? For girls they're an excuse for posh dresses and getting mushy. For lads they're a reason to party. For the two lovers here it was something much more intimate.

👁 Read 3 v 6 – 4 v 7

ENGAGE YOUR BRAIN

▶ How did she picture her husband on their wedding day? (3 v 11)

▶ How would you sum up the man's compliments (4 v 1–7) in modern language?

Ever pictured yourself as bride or groom in a royal wedding? That's what the woman's doing — imagining her husband as the great King Solomon on his wedding day.

👁 Read 4 v 8 – 5 v 1

▶ What other qualities does he mention? (v9–11)

▶ What do you think they're both talking about with their strange images? (4 v 12, 5 v 1)

The focus now is on their wedding night — they've been longing to get their hands on each other for ages. In v12–14, he describes her as a

fruitful garden (ripe to be enjoyed) and locked up (pure, a virgin) and a fountain waiting to break open. And in 5 v 1 the waiting is over. Nothing shameful or embarrassing here: a husband and wife giving themselves to each other without inhibition. And their friends say: Go on, you two, enjoy it.

This steamy section throws away the myth that Christians hate sex. The Bible says it's right for a husband and wife to enjoy each other physically. Sex is God's wedding present. What an awesome God!

PRAY ABOUT IT

Ask God to give you the right attitude towards love, marriage and sex. Ask Him to help you properly respect the opposite sex. And ask for His help in saving sex for marriage.

→ TAKE IT FURTHER

Words of wisdom from Jesus can be found on page 113.

29 | Song of frustration

Relationships are hard work. Even this marriage we're reading about. They're so in love and yet there are still misunderstandings, worries and problems.

👁 Read Song of Songs 5 v 2–8

The man is late home from work and looking forward to cuddling up with his wife. But she's been sleeping and recently washed and doesn't feel in the mood. Yet soon her heart is beating fast for him again. But it's too late — he's frustrated and has left.

ENGAGE YOUR BRAIN

▶ *How does she feel? (v6)*

▶ *What happens to her? (v7)*

The initial excitement of marriage has worn off a little and she is taking him for granted. But she soon regrets it and goes looking for the man. We must be careful not to take our relationships for granted. Especially our relationship with Jesus. He offers us so much — be careful not to throw it back in His face.

👁 Read 5 v 9 – 6 v 3

▶ *What do her friends ask? (v9)*

▶ *How does she feel about her man? (v10–16)*

She really does love him. To her, he is perfect — she just loves the way he looks. And when she thinks about it, she knows where he has gone (6 v 1–3) — to do some gardening, of course! In a relationship, we must appreciate the good things about the other person. And let them know they're wanted.

PRAY ABOUT IT

That goes for our relationship with Jesus too. Spend time now praying, focusing on the things that amaze you about Him.

→ TAKE IT FURTHER

Encore on page 113.

30 | Song of passion

Once the wedding's over and you slip into routine, love goes dull, doesn't it? Well, I hope you don't believe that lie. Love needn't go cold. Get the fiery passion of this next section...

👁 Read Song of Songs 6 v 4–13

ENGAGE YOUR BRAIN

ⅅ How would you summarise his feelings towards her? (v4–9)

Yet again the man showers his wife with compliments. Here's a lesson guys — women don't usually tire of hearing compliments! There's never a time in a relationship when you should stop building up your partner (yes, that goes for females, too).

👁 Read 7 v 1–9

He's getting quite excited now and can't get enough of her. His descriptions and desires are very intimate. This is the right place for sexual desire, within marriage. And it's important for a husband and wife to enjoy each other's bodies as well as everything else about each other.

👁 Read 7 v 9 – 8 v 4

ⅅ What does she long to do with her man?
7 v 11–12:

8 v 1:
8 v 2:

ⅅ What warning comes up again in 8 v 4?

She feels totally secure with him (just as we should feel secure in our relationship with God). She longs to get him alone. And she wishes she could kiss him in public, but that wasn't socially acceptable.

The right place to awaken sexual feelings (v4) is marriage. Our sex drive can be so strong it's dangerous to stir it up in someone outside of marriage. So think: *"How can I please God?"* not *"What can I get away with?"*

PRAY ABOUT IT

Talk to God about issues and struggles and longings that are on your mind today.

→ TAKE IT FURTHER

More love stuff on page 113.

31 | Song of celebration

It's been an eye-opening book. Let's take one last look at love and desire as God has created them to be enjoyed.

👁 Read Song of Songs 8 v 5–7

ENGAGE YOUR BRAIN

▶ *What different things does the woman recognise about love?*

When love comes, it's irresistible and incredibly powerful. It's valuable too. So don't treat it lightly. And be careful — love and sexual desire can be overpowering so save them for the right time and circumstances.

👁 Read verses 8–14

▶ *What had the friends worried about the woman when she was younger? (v8–9)*

▶ *Can love be bought? (v11–12)*

When she was young, they'd worried. Would she be a "wall" and save her body for marriage? Or would she be a "door", allowing someone in to take her virginity too early? Verse 10 tells us she saved herself for marriage — and it was worth it.

As the song ends, we're reminded that love cannot be bought (v11–12, and neither should sex be bought). And then the love poem ends on a positive note — the couple longing for each other. And that's Song of Songs: the best love song of them all.

Now let's look at the bigger picture. Those who trust in Jesus know a love that's stronger, deeper and purer than human sexual love. Marriage points us to Christ's perfect, sacrificial love for His church (Christians). He has shown His passion for His people to win them back: a love that led to the cross. One day, Jesus will bring His people into His presence forever. And there will be the biggest wedding celebration ever!

THINK IT OVER

▶ *How has Song of Songs changed your view of God sex and marriage?*

TAKE IT FURTHER

A tiny bit more on page 114.

32 ┆ A Massah-ve problem

You know how people often tell us to read our Bibles regularly? Today's psalm says that doing that can be very, very dangerous...

👁 Read Psalm 95

This psalm's reminding God's people about a time when their ancestors were travelling from Egypt (where God rescued them) to Israel (the land God had promised them). As they went, God spoke to them at places like Meribah and Massah.

ENGAGE YOUR BRAIN

▷ *How did they respond to hearing God? (v8–9)*

▷ *How did God respond? (v10)*

▷ *What was the outcome? (v11)*

"Rest" was what God was offering in the land He'd promised: enjoying life lived God's way in God's land. But many of those who called themselves God's people never got there, because instead of listening and obeying God, they listened and ignored Him.

THINK IT THROUGH

▷ *What's the big lesson for us to learn today? (v7–8)*

▷ *What do we need to do every time we read or listen to God's voice in the Bible?*

▷ *What are we encouraged to do in v1–2 and v6?*

▷ *What reasons for doing this are given? (v3–7)*

GET ON WITH IT

Question is: will you obey? Will you bow down before God; will you worship Him in how you live; will you sing and speak to Him about how great He is? Or will you harden your heart?

THE BOTTOM LINE

Don't just listen to God: obey Him in your heart and in your life.

→ TAKE IT FURTHER

More problems on page 114.

33 | I'm so excited...

The guy who wrote this song is seriously excited about... God! Let's dig in to see why: hopefully we'll find that, by the end of this psalm, we're excited too.

👁 Read Psalm 96 v 1–6

ENGAGE YOUR BRAIN

▷ *What should we do? (v1–2)*

▷ *Why? (v4–6)*

▷ *How does the LORD compare to anything else people worship? (v5)*

Every day we have a choice: to worship the One who made everything, or worship a "god" that's made up. We can live for money, or popularity, or exam success, or sex: or we can live for the awesome, ruling, creator God.

GET ON WITH IT

▷ *Who should be hearing about this amazing God? (v3)*

▷ *Who could you try to tell about God today?*

👁 Read verses 7–13

Verses 7–9 are addressed to "all the earth". Every single human ought to recognise God's glory, offer Him their best, and seek to live with Him now so they can live with Him eternally.

Verses 10-13 are about the future.

▷ *What will the whole of creation do one day? (v11–12)*

▷ *Why? (v13)*

Excited? You should be! One day, everything in creation will praise God for His justice and His rule. Today, you can bring that future into your present by praising your God in all that you do and say.

PRAY ABOUT IT

Re-read this psalm, then spend some time thanking God for who He is. You can even sing it, if you want!

TAKE IT FURTHER

Excited? Read more on page 114.

34 | Terrifying or terrific?

God's coming back! In Psalm 96, that truth is great news — but in today's psalm we see there's another side to the story.

👁 Read Psalm 97 v 1–7

ENGAGE YOUR BRAIN

▷ *What picture of God do we get in v2–6?*

▷ *How does this description make you feel?*

▷ *What kind of people is this a problem for? (v3, 7)*

This should terrify us. We all sometimes treat something other than the real God as our god. We all sometimes think something other than God will give us what we need in life — we "boast in idols" (v7). But…

👁 Read verses 8–12

▷ *Who is able to "rejoice" about God's return? (v8, 11–12)*

"Zion" means "all God's people". How can we be part of God's righteous family? The New Testament explains: "God made [Jesus] who had no sin to be sin for us, so that in him we might become the righteousness of God" (2 Corinthians 5 v 21). It's through trusting in Jesus and His death that you and I can be made right with God.

▷ *How does that make you feel?*

▷ *According to v10, how can we show we love this awesome, rescuing God?*

GET ON WITH IT

▷ *Whatever else happens in your day, what does this psalm tell you that you can rejoice about?*

THE BOTTOM LINE

Jesus' death means His return will be terrific, not terrifying, for believers.

→ TAKE IT FURTHER

More terrific news on page 114.

Is Christianity only for weak people?

"Yes!" says one of Britain's leading scientists, Stephen Hawking: "Heaven is a fairy story for people afraid of the dark." Christians are just people who aren't brave enough to admit that this life is all there is — that there's no God looking out for us, no great purpose to life, no heaven beyond death. They're just weak. Aren't they? Well, no. And yes. And no. Let me explain…

NO

It would be a bit weak to believe in God without any evidence. It would be weak to make up an afterlife so we could feel better. But what if the facts pointed to the existence of God and the reality of an afterlife?

When, on the first Easter Sunday, some women went to the tomb of their dead friend Jesus, they didn't find His body. Instead, they found some angels, who told them: *"He has risen! Remember how he told you … 'The Son of Man must be delivered into the hands of sinful men, be crucified and on the third day be raised again.' Then they remembered his words."* (Luke 24 v 6–8).

The fact of Jesus' resurrection proves that He is who He said He was: God. It proves that what He says about life, death and life beyond death is true. Christianity stands or falls on the reality of the resurrection. If it didn't happen, Christians are weak, *"to be pitied more than all men"* (1 Corinthians 15 v 19). *"But Christ has indeed been raised from the dead"* (v 20) — and He gave us loads of evidence to prove it. Christians aren't people who believe in Jesus in spite of the facts: we believe because of the facts.

It's not weak to follow the facts. It's not weak to say: "If Jesus rose from the dead, I need to listen to what He says, instead of thinking I know better". People who laugh at

Christians for being weak don't tend to deal with the resurrection, or come up with a different explanation. They often dismiss or ignore it, without considering the evidence.

YES

And yet, Christianity *is* for weak people. The Bible says we are all "sick", in desperate need of help. Jesus Himself said: *"It is not the healthy who need a doctor, but the sick. I have not come to call the righteous* [those who think they've got their lives sorted] *but sinners* [those who know they haven't]" (Mark 2 v 17).

Every human is a sinner, a rebel against God. Since God is our life-giver and ruler, that leaves us *"dead in your transgressions and sins ... by nature objects of wrath"* (Ephesians 2 v 1, 3). Spiritually dead... facing God's anger... you can't get much weaker than that! But Jesus said He came to be a "doctor" to the spiritually sick. On the cross, He took God's anger in our place, and offered us His perfect life: *"By his wounds we are healed"* (Isaiah 53 v 5).

That's amazing news: but we'll only realise it's amazing if we first realise we need Jesus to heal us. It takes guts to accept you're weak and need help: it takes guts to stop ignoring your sickness, and turn to Jesus for healing.

NO

This is how Jesus describes the Christian life: *"If anyone would come after me, he must deny himself and take up his cross and follow me. For whoever wants to save his life will lose it, but whoever loses his life for me and for the gospel will save it"* (Mark 8 v 34–35).

Followers of Jesus sign up for a life which ends in eternal life, but which will involve self-denial, suffering and even death before that. Living as a Christian means we don't do what is easiest for us, what we feel like, what others expect. Instead we follow Jesus, wherever it takes us. Christianity is not an easy option: it makes life tougher.

The weak option is to hear what Jesus says and decide following Him is too hard. The difficult, courageous choice is to realise that Jesus is the risen Lord; realise you need Him to save you; and give your whole life to Him. There's nothing weak about that.

Matthew

Follow the leader

According to legend, the great British polar explorer, Ernest Shackleton, placed an advert in a newspaper before his expedition. "Men wanted for a hazardous journey. Small wages, bitter cold. Long months of complete darkness. Constant danger, safe return doubtful. Honour and recognition in case of success." He received more than 5,000 applications.

If you were to write an advert for joining Jesus' team, then chapters 8–14 of Matthew's Gospel would be a good place to start. However, they would give you an equally mixed idea of what to expect!

The hazards are personal cost, opposition, people trying to mislead you, and persecution, even to death. But the benefits include forgiveness, close relationship with the God who created you, His Spirit in you, eternal life, and God's care for you every day. The big question is: will you trust your leader? It's a hazardous journey but travelling with Jesus guarantees our safe arrival, and our eternal reward.

The disciples are slowly learning what it means to have faith in Jesus; to find rest in Him; to focus on Him and not the things they fear. We'll see that He is the centre of history, — the One promised all through the Old Testament. The only One who can open our eyes to see God.

And sadly, we'll see a lot of people on the outside; people rejecting Jesus and facing the bitter cold and complete darkness of being without their true leader and King.

Are you ready to follow your leader?

35 ┊ Healing power ┊

Three healing episodes follow the famous Sermon on the Mount, but what are they revealing about Jesus?

👁 **Read Matthew 8 v 1–4**

ENGAGE YOUR BRAIN

▶ *What is the man's problem in v2?*
▶ *How does Jesus respond? (v3)*

Jesus' command (v4) showed His respect for the Old Testament. It would also restore the man back to society and the priests would hear of Jesus' power over illness.

👁 **Read verses 5–13**

▶ *What is the centurion's problem? (v6)*
▶ *Remember he's an enemy Roman, yet how does Jesus respond to his request? (v7)*
▶ *What's so amazing about the centurion's faith? What does he recognise about Jesus? (v8–9)*
▶ *What's the outcome? (v13)*

Jesus reminds His listeners here that the kingdom of heaven is the same kingdom promised to Abraham, Isaac and Jacob — a kingdom you enter by faith (v10–12).

👁 **Read verses 14–17**

▶ *What's the illness Jesus deals with in v14?*
▶ *What's the woman's response to Jesus? (v15)*

Matthew points us to Isaiah, one of the greatest Old Testament prophets, to explain what Jesus is doing (v17).

PRAY ABOUT IT

Thank Jesus that He is both willing and able to heal us. Thank Him for His death on the cross, that makes us clean. Ask Him to give you eyes to see your sinfulness and faith to enter His kingdom.

THE BOTTOM LINE

Jesus is the living, loving, powerful, fulfilment of the Old Testament.

→ **TAKE IT FURTHER**

More from Isaiah on page 115.

36 | No compromise

Have you ever volunteered for something only to realise when the time comes to actually do it that... it's raining, there's something really good on TV, no one you know will be there, or it's going to be too much like hard work?

👁 Read Matthew 8 v 18–22

ENGAGE YOUR BRAIN

▶ What do these two guys have in common? (v19 & 21)

▶ What is Jesus' answer to the first man? (v20)

▶ What about the second man?

▶ What are the two men putting ahead of their desire to follow Jesus?

▶ What about you? What gets in the way of your following Jesus whole-heartedly?

For some of us it might be physical comfort, or material possessions, like the first guy. Jesus won't necessarily ask us to sleep rough as He did, but would you be prepared to? Or maybe, like the second disciple, it's your family relationships, or your friends holding you back. Maybe a boyfriend or girlfriend? (Just to say, Jesus isn't

being really cold here as if the guy's father has only just died. The sense of the man's request is that he wants to wait until his parents have grown old and died before he's free to leave and follow Jesus.)

PRAY ABOUT IT

Be really honest with yourself and with Jesus (He already knows anyway!). What's stopping you following Him properly today? Ask Him to help you to follow Him.

GET ON WITH IT

And what are you going to do as a result? It might be painful; in fact it probably will be. But take a look ahead to Matthew 16 v 24–26.

THE BOTTOM LINE

Following Jesus is costly, but the reward is priceless.

→ TAKE IT FURTHER

Find some more on page 115.

37 | Storming stuff

Have you ever been really frightened? Actually feared for your life? If so, you'll know just how the disciples felt here.

👁 **Read Matthew 8 v 23–27**

ENGAGE YOUR BRAIN

▷ *How bad was this storm?*

▷ *What's right about the disciples' reaction? (v25)*

▷ *What's wrong? (v26)*

Let's not forget that at least four of the disciples were fishermen. They'd seen bad storms before, and this one was obviously pretty serious. And at least they turn to the one person who can help, but Jesus is disappointed by their lack of faith. Think of it this way — they are in the safest place in the world, with the one who not only commands the wind and waves but created them.

▷ *Why are the disciples so amazed? (v26–27)*

Even after a storm is over it takes a while for the waves to die down. Jesus simply speaks and everything is instantly calm. In the account of this episode in Mark's Gospel, the word Jesus uses to calm the storm is the sort of thing you would say to a family dog – "Sit"!

▷ *Read Psalm 107 v 23–32 and see if you can answer the question the disciples ask in v27.*

PRAY ABOUT IT

Have you recognised who Jesus really is? Talk to Him now about the things that scare you.

THE BOTTOM LINE

Who is this man?

➡ **TAKE IT FURTHER**

A glimpse of the future on page 115.

38 Pigging out

The kingdom of heaven will be free from sin, sickness and chaos. It will also, importantly, be free from evil. Check out pig-gate to see the King in action!

👁 Read Matthew 8 v 28–32

ENGAGE YOUR BRAIN

▷ *Who does Jesus encounter in v28? What are they like?*

▷ *What do they recognise about Jesus?*

▷ *What do the evil spirits know will happen to them? (v29)*

▷ *What happens to them in v32?*

Jesus has a zero-tolerance approach to evil. However threatening or scary these things can seem, Jesus is more than able to deal with evil.

PRAY ABOUT IT

Christians should remind each other that the devil is defeated but not yet destroyed. (Check out Ephesians 6 v 10–20 and also Ephesians 1 v 18–23). Remember that although we are living with spiritual opposition, our King Jesus has triumphed and reigns over everything.

👁 Read verses 33–34

▷ *Is the town's reaction to these events surprising?*

▷ *Why do you think they react this way?*

▷ *How might you have expected them to respond?*

TALK IT OVER

Chat to an older Christian about the idea of evil and demons if it confuses or unsettles you. Perhaps it all seems a bit unbelievable — but the New Testament is quite clear, both that evil forces exist, and also that Jesus is far more powerful. Romans 8 v 38–39 is a brilliant passage to learn by heart!

THE BOTTOM LINE

Jesus has defeated the devil.

→ TAKE IT FURTHER

Pig out on page 115.

39 | Power point

If you've broken your leg, you need an ambulance, not a bunch of flowers, right? In this next episode it looks as if Jesus has lost his marbles to begin with...

👁 Read Matthew 9 v 1–2

ENGAGE YOUR BRAIN

- ▶ *What is the man's problem?*
- ▶ *How does Jesus respond? (v2)*
- ▶ *How would you describe the way He speaks to the man?*
- ▶ *What does this show us about Jesus?*
- ▶ *What does Jesus see as the man's biggest need?*
- ▶ *Does the paralysed man do anything?*

That last one was a bit of a trick question — obviously the man can't do anything, he's paralysed! Plus it was his friends that brought him — Jesus responds to their faith, not the man's. But this man isn't just physically helpless: he is spiritually helpless too. He needs God's forgiveness and Jesus gives it to him.

👁 Read verses 3–8

- ▶ *Why do the teachers of the law react the way they do? (v3)*
- ▶ *Who can forgive all our sins?*

- ▶ *What is Jesus claiming about Himself?*
- ▶ *Which do you think is easier to say and why? (v5)*
- ▶ *How does Jesus prove His authority? (v6–7)*
- ▶ *What is the crowd's reaction?*
- ▶ *Have they got the big picture about Jesus yet?*

Of course it's easier to say your sins are forgiven — nobody can tell whether that's happened, but Jesus shows His power and authority by doing the visible miracle too. But which is easier to do? Healing someone was a piece of cake compared to going to the cross so that our sins could be forgiven.

PRAY ABOUT IT

Thank Jesus that He went to the cross so that we could be forgiven; that He did the hard thing that we could never do.

→ TAKE IT FURTHER

Power over to page 115.

40 Doctor and bridegroom

Ever wondered who this guy Matthew was, who wrote this Gospel? Well, it's more than likely he's the same man we meet now in v9.

Read Matthew 9 v 9–13
▷ *What was Matthew's job? (v9)*
▷ *What does Jesus say to him?*
▷ *And his reaction?*

Tax collectors were usually corrupt money-grabbers who, worst of all, colluded with the enemy Romans. Nice followers you pick, eh Jesus? And having dinner with him and his shady mates too? At least, that's what the Pharisees were saying.

▷ *How does Jesus explain His behaviour? (v12)*
▷ *What do the Pharisees need to work out? (v13)*

Bit of an insult there for the Pharisees, who thought they were super holy. They hadn't understood the Old Testament at all. Jesus looks at people's hearts, not their outward behaviour, and we all need open heart surgery.

Read verses 14–17
▷ *What is John's disciples' issue with Jesus' followers? (v14)*
▷ *Why was fasting not appropriate for Jesus' disciples? (v15)*
▷ *What do you think Jesus is getting at in v16–17?*

Jesus is saying that you can't apply old rules to something new. Yes, Jesus is the fulfilment of the Old Testament, but the trailer is not the film. Something amazing and new is happening and a whole new way of doing things is inevitable now that Jesus is here.

PRAY ABOUT IT
Have you ever honestly admitted to Jesus that you're spiritually sick and need Him to be your doctor? Thank Him that He came for sinners.

THE BOTTOM LINE
Jesus came to call sinners.

→ TAKE IT FURTHER
Revelations on page 115.

41 | Healing words

How do people react to Jesus? Are they respectful? Patronising? Indifferent? Hostile? What about your friends and family? What about you?

👁 Read Matthew 9 v 18–34

ENGAGE YOUR BRAIN

▶ *What is Jesus asked to do? (v18)*
▶ *How much does this ruler trust Jesus?*
▶ *Is he justified in doing so? (v25)*

That is serious faith. But it's not over the top if Jesus is the Son of God.

▶ *Who else is seeking a miracle from Jesus? (v20–21)*
▶ *Is she as upfront as the ruler?*
▶ *How does Jesus treat her? (v22)*

That gentle, encouraging word again (see v2). "Take heart, daughter, your faith has healed you." Jesus wants us to trust Him. However timidly we try, He accepts us with love and encouragement.

▶ *Do the blind men show faith in Jesus? (v27–30)*
▶ *Is the mute demon-possessed man able to contribute anything to his cure?*

▶ *How does the crowd respond to all these miracles? (v33)*
▶ *And the Pharisees? (v34)*
▶ *Why is their response so terrible?*

It's almost unbelievable that the Pharisees could get it so wrong. It's a serious case of sour grapes but with a terminal outcome. If you reject the rescuer, you cannot be rescued...

PRAY ABOUT IT

Powerful, death-defying, yet gentle and loving. Thank God that we have such a great King!

SHARE IT

Ask someone today what their response to Jesus is. If they say they don't know, challenge them to read a Gospel (keep some yourself to give away) and then get back to you.

→ TAKE IT FURTHER

Quick! Go to page 115!

42 | Mission possible

A new phase in Matthew's Gospel starts here. Jesus, the one with unique authority in teaching (chapters 5–7) and miracles (chapters 8–9), hands authority on to His disciples. They're sent out to continue His mission.

👁 Read Matthew 9 v 35–38

ENGAGE YOUR BRAIN

ⓘ How does v35 sum up Jesus' mission?

ⓘ What is Jesus' attitude towards the crowds? (v36)

ⓘ Why is it so bad for sheep to be without a shepherd?

ⓘ Who is ultimately responsible for the success of God's growing kingdom? (v38)

PRAY ABOUT IT

Do you see non-Christians ("the lost") in this way — like sheep without a shepherd? Ask Jesus to help you have His compassion for the lost, and pray verse 38!

👁 Read Matthew 10 v 1–15

ⓘ Who sends out the twelve? (v1)

ⓘ How does Jesus describe the people the disciples would be preaching to? (v6)

ⓘ What are the disciples to do? (v7–8)

ⓘ Do you think it will all be straightforward for them? (v14)

We know that Jesus' mission is for the whole world and He certainly hasn't shown any bias against non-Jews (look back at chapter 8 v 10–11), but He wants His disciples to start with Israel. God's plan in the Old Testament was to bless the world through His chosen people (see Genesis 12 v 3).

THE BOTTOM LINE

People without Jesus are like sheep without a shepherd.

→ TAKE IT FURTHER

Follow the flock to page 116.

43 ┊ Christians in conflict ┊

Jesus sent His disciples to continue His mission.
Now He spells out exactly what that work involves.
And that spelling reads C-O-N-F-L-I-C-T. Christians
should expect exactly the same.

👁 Read Matthew 10 v 16–31

ENGAGE YOUR BRAIN

▶ What should characterise the
disciples as they set out on their
good-news-sharing mission? (v16)

▶ What will they encounter?
(v17–23)

▶ What is Jesus' warning in v17?

▶ Why shouldn't they be surprised
by all this opposition? (v24–25)

▶ What is Jesus' next piece of
advice? (v26)

▶ Why can the disciples react this
way? (v26–31) List the reasons.

-
-
-

Following in Jesus' footsteps will
mean persecution. But we, like the
first disciples, are to expect that.

Don't forget to spot the promises too
(v20, 30). God, our heavenly Father,
is with us by His Spirit.

PRAY ABOUT IT

Who or what are you fearing today?
Man or God (v28)? Are you more
concerned about being teased or
rejected than standing firm for Jesus?
Ask for the Holy Spirit's help to have
a healthy fear of God today wherever
you find yourself.

TALK IT THROUGH

Do you really expect to suffer as
a follower of Jesus? Why? Why
not? Get together with a Christian
friend and think about how you can
encourage each other to stand firm
without being afraid.

→ TAKE IT FURTHER

Fight on to page 116.

55

44 | Faith fight

Do you ever hear people saying that Jesus was a peacemaker? Well that's partly true, but this next section shows that He could also be the opposite!

👁 Read Matthew 10 v 32–33

ENGANGE YOUR BRAIN

▷ *Is v32–33 fair?*
▷ *How does it make you feel?*

Hands up if you're feeling guilty/panicked? Don't get things out of perspective — look ahead to chapter 12 v 20; Jesus will not break a bruised reed or snuff out a smouldering candle: He knows that we are weak. Peter, a key disciple, denied knowing Jesus as He faced the cross but was restored and forgiven after the resurrection. This verse, in fact this whole section, is about loyalties.

👁 Read verses 34–39

▷ *What does Jesus say about His mission? (v34)*
▷ *Does this surprise you?*
▷ *Would it surprise your non-Christian friends?*
▷ *What is your reaction to v35–39?*

The amazing thing about v37 is that none of us is worthy of Christ. And

because of that, He went to the cross. He lost His life so we could find ours. But if we are to follow Him, we need to give up everything that might come between us and Jesus. You cannot be winched to safety by a rescue helicopter if you are still clinging to the shipwreck. We need to hold onto Jesus with both hands.

👁 Read verses 40–42

▷ *What is the result of holding onto Jesus?*
▷ *What do you think this reward is? (Clue v32, v39)*

PRAY ABOUT IT

Is your first loyalty to Christ? Look back at what He did for you at the cross and ask for His help to live full on for Him today.

THE BOTTOM LINE

Jesus comes first.

→ TAKE IT FURTHER

More controversial stuff on page 116.

45 | Identity parade

How would you identify someone famous? There might be little clues like bodyguards or a car with flags on. Here, John the Baptist's disciples are trying to identify Jesus, and Jesus in turn tells people how to identify John.

👁 **Read Matthew 11 v 1–6**

ENGAGE YOUR BRAIN

▷ What do John's followers want to know about Jesus? (v3)

▷ What clues does Jesus give to His identity? (v4–5)

If you were familiar with your Old Testament, what Jesus was doing were signs screaming out "THIS IS THE MESSIAH!" Check out Isaiah 61 v 1–3. Jesus is the one who was promised; we shouldn't expect anyone else (v3). That's why all these so-called modern prophets or cult leaders are clearly frauds.

PRAY ABOUT IT

Even John the Baptist was a little unsure and wanted reassurance about who Jesus is. Thank God for the evidence He gives us, and pray for yourself or anyone you know who suffers doubts about their faith from time to time.

👁 **Read verses 7–19**

▷ What does Jesus ask the crowd about John? (v7–9)

▷ Who does Jesus say John is?
v9:
v10:
v14:

▷ What criticism does Jesus have of the generation who saw both John and Jesus? (v16)

Like kids in an argumentative mood, Jesus' audience was never satisfied. John the Baptist was too severe for them; Jesus was too free and easy. But notice v19. John's actions show who he was just as Jesus' do.

SHARE IT

All the evidence stacks up to show that Jesus is God's King. Ask God to help you share Jesus' identity with someone this week.

➡ **TAKE IT FURTHER**
I.D. check on page 116.

Smuggling for God

Andy van der Bijl, who became known as Brother Andrew, was born in 1928, the third of six children who lived in the smallest house in the village of Witte in the Netherlands. It was a tough childhood, with his brother Bas dying when Andrew was just 11.

His thirst for adventure led him into the Dutch army at the age of 18, where he became a notorious commando. The atrocities that Andrew committed as a commando haunted him and he became wrapped in guilt. Nothing he did — drinking, fighting, writing or reading letters — helped him escape the stranglehold that guilt had on him. Shot in the ankle in combat, at the age of 20, his time in the army came to an abrupt end. In hospital, he started to read a Bible given to him by a nurse.

Unable to walk properly, Andrew returned to his old town, his life seeming empty. But his thirst for God grew. Every evening, Andrew attended a Christian meeting and during the day he would read the Bible. At last, one evening, he prayed: "Lord, if You will show me the way, I will follow You."

Soon after becoming a Christian, Andrew knew God was calling him to become a missionary. He travelled to Scotland to study at Bible college and, after graduating, he went on a trip to Czechoslovakia with the Communist Party. Andy managed to break away from the organised trip to learn that the church in Czechoslovakia was suffering and that Bibles were very rare. Officials were angry he had broken away from the official tour and had contact with Christians so he was banned from entering the country again.

But this trip had opened his eyes to the needs of the church behind the "iron curtain" and this became his mission field. God provided Andrew with a new Volkswagen Beetle car, and with it he smuggled Bibles and literature into countries where Christianity was not welcome. During this time, communist countries were keeping a tight control on their borders, and Andrew tells many nerve-wracking stories.

"When I pulled up to the checkpoint in Romania, I said to myself, 'Well, I'm in luck. Only six cars. This border crossing should go swiftly.' But when it took forty minutes to inspect the first car, I began to worry ... literally everything that family was carrying had to be taken out and spread on the ground. Every car in line was put through the same routine.

"I prayed: 'Lord, any serious inspection will show up these Romanian Bibles immediately. Let me take some of the Bibles out and leave them in the open where they will be seen. Then, Lord, I can't possibly be depending on my own abilities, can I? I'll be depending entirely on You.'

"While the last car was going through its chilling inspection, I took several Bibles from their hiding places and piled them on the seat beside me. Then it was my turn. I inched the car up to the officer standing at the side of the road, handed him my papers, and started to get out. But his knee was against the door, holding it closed. He looked at my photograph in the passport, scribbled something down, shoved the papers back under my nose, and abruptly waved me on.

"I started the engine. Was I supposed to pull over, out of the way where the car could be taken apart? I coasted forward, my foot poised above the brake. Nothing happened. I looked out the rear mirror. The guard was waving the next car to stop, indicating to the driver to get out. On I drove a few more yards. The guard was having the driver behind me open the hood of his car. And then I was too far away to doubt that I had made it through that incredible checkpoint in the space of thirty seconds. My heart was racing. Not with the excitement of the crossing, but with the excitement of having caught such a spectacular glimpse of God at work!"

Brother Andrew founded Open Doors, which continues to work in many countries, distributing Bibles, training pastors, teaching people to read using the Bible and many other great things. To find out more, check out www.opendoorsuk.org or www.opendoorsusa.org. Or get hold of *God's Smuggler* from a Christian bookshop.

46 ¦ 1 Kings: Ruling passion

God's people, the Israelites, have split into two nations. King Rehoboam rules Judah in the south and King Jeroboam rules Israel in the north. Time for some astonishing stories from foolish Jeroboam's reign...

Read 1 Kings 12 v 25–33

ENGAGE YOUR BRAIN

▷ *Why did Jeroboam make the golden calves? (v26–29)*

This king was bad news. He broke the unity of God's people; he set up idols; he diverted people away from God's temple; he restored the high places; he made anyone a priest, against God's law; he re-arranged God's calendar of festivals; and he took the priest's role himself. No wonder he forfeited the promise God had made to him (11 v 38).

Read 13 v 1–10, 33–34

▷ *How was God's power shown? (v4–6)*

▷ *What effect did these miracles have on evil Jeroboam? (v33–34)*

God gave the king a chance to change his ways but, amazingly, he refused. We must be careful not to ignore God's warnings when He gives us the chance to turn back to Him.

Read verses 11–34

▷ *What did the old prophet do wrong? (v18)*

▷ *What did the man of God do wrong? (v19–22)*

▷ *What happened? (v24)*

This is a weird story and quite baffling. But the bottom line seems to be this: disobey God and He will punish you. And we need to watch out for people who claim to teach God's word but are lying. Check what you hear with what the Bible says.

PRAY ABOUT IT

Pray for people you know who refuse to turn back to God. Pray for Christian leaders that they'd teach God's word correctly and faithfully.

THE BOTTOM LINE

Disobey God and He'll punish you.

→ TAKE IT FURTHER

No *Take it further* today.

47 | The name game

Don't get confused by names today. Jeroboam was the evil king of Israel and Rehoboam was the evil king of Judah. Both had sons called Abijah. Oh, and there was a prophet with the confusingly similar name of Ahijah.

Read 1 Kings 14 v 1–20

ENGAGE YOUR BRAIN

▶ *What was the sad situation? (v1)*
▶ *What was God's message to Jeroboam? (v7–11)*
▶ *What were the results of Jeroboam's sin? (v12, 14–16)*

God won't tolerate it when we worship anything other than Him. And our sin often affects other people, not just ourselves. Because of Jeroboam's sin and idolatry, his son died and the whole nation of Israel was punished.

Read verses 21–31

▶ *What did the people of Judah do wrong? (v22–24)*
▶ *How did God punish them? (v25–26)*
▶ *What was happening between God's people in Israel and Judah? (v30)*
▶ *What fact is mentioned in both v21 and v31?*
▶ *Who took over from Rehob? (v31)*

Jerusalem was God's city, with God's name attached to it (v21). But the people there turned from God to the disgusting worship of other gods. So the Lord let Egypt invade and carry away much of the wealth He had given to King Solomon.

It seems odd that the king's mother gets mentioned twice. But the fact she was an Ammonite shows how God's people were being influenced by their godless neighbours, who worshipped false gods.

THINK IT OVER

▶ *How do you let non-Christians influence you in negative ways?*
▶ *How does your sin affect other people?*
▶ *What do you need to do to stick closer to God?*

Answer these questions honestly and then ask for God's help in your life.

→ TAKE IT FURTHER

Fast forward to page 117.

48 | A tale of two kings

After rotten Rehoboam died, his son and then grandson were the next two kings of Judah. Would Abijah abide by God's rules? Would Asa be an ace king?

👁 Read 1 Kings 15 v 1–8

ENGAGE YOUR BRAIN
▶ What was Abijah like? (v3)

▶ Yet what did God do for him and why? (v4–5)

We're not told much about King Abijah and almost everything we're told is bad. He disobeyed God and followed the disgusting ways of his father, Rehoboam. The only good thing he had going for him was that God graciously give him a son. God kept His promise to David. God always keeps His promises, no matter how bad things are.

👁 Read verse 9–24
▶ How was Asa different from his dad, Abijah? (v11)

▶ What good things did he do?
v12:
v13:
v14:
v15:

▶ How did he protect Judah's security? (v18–20)

At last, a king who pleased God! He did this by destroying all the bad stuff in his nation (v12). He wasn't perfect — he didn't get rid of all the "high places" (that might be used for idol worship) and he made a pact with an evil king. But his heart was committed to God, and that's what counts.

GET ON WITH IT
▶ Is your heart committed to serving the Lord?

▶ What idols and bad things do you need to throw out of your life to show your commitment to God?

THE BOTTOM LINE
Throw out idols and commit your heart to God.

→ TAKE IT FURTHER
More tales on page 117.

Bad, bad, bad, bad, bad

The focus is back on the northern kingdom of Israel.
Remember, these are God's chosen people we're
reading about, but you wouldn't know it by the way
they behaved. And their kings went from bad to worse.

Read 1 Kings 15 v 25 – 16 v 7

ENGAGE YOUR BRAIN

- *What effect did King Nadab have on the people? (v26)*
- *What did Baasha do? (v27–29)*
- *Why was Jeroboam and Nadab's family destroyed? (v30)*
- *What kind of king was Baasha? (v34)*
- *So what would God do? (v2–3)*

God always keeps His word. After
Jeroboam led Israel in sin, God
promised to destroy His family.
The Lord used Baasha to do this, but
Baasha was just as bad, even though
God had made him king (16 v 2).
So the same fate awaited Baasha
and his family.

Read 1 Kings 16 v 8–28

- *What happened to Elah? (v9–10)*
- *Did God keep His earlier promise to Baasha? (v12–13)*
- *How long was Zimri king? (v15)*
- *What happened to him? (v16–18)*
- *Why? (v19)*

- *How did Omri compare with the other kings? (v25–26)*

How depressing! King after king led
the Israelites in worshipping idols and
rejecting God. Despite all this, God
was still in control and hadn't given
up on His people.

THE BOTTOM LINE

God is always in control and always
keeps His promises.

PRAY ABOUT IT

Thank God for these great truths
about Him, praising Him for specific
promises He has made to His people.
Pray that you would let Him be in
control of your life, walking in His
ways every day.

→ TAKE IT FURTHER

More dirt on Baasha on page 117.

50 | Ahab vs Elijah

The kings of Israel were going from bad to worse. And none were more evil then Ahab. But there was good news at last — God raised up His prophet, Elijah, to stand up to evil Ahab. Get ready for some incredible events.

👁 Read 16 v 29 – 17 v 24

ENGAGE YOUR BRAIN

▶ *What was Ahab's attitude to disobeying God? (v30–31)*

▶ *Why was his marriage to Jezebel a disastrous move? (v31)*

▶ *What else did Ahab do? (32–33)*

▶ *What was the surprising message from God? (17 v 1)*

▶ *How did God look after Elijah?*

👁 Read 1 Kings 17 v 7–16

Sidon (v9) was where Jezebel, Ahab's wife, came from. God sent Elijah into foreign territory — where Baal was worshipped. God was in charge outside Israel as well as inside it, and He looked after both His prophet and this non-Israelite family.

👁 Read verses 17–24

▶ *What was the crisis? (v17)*

▶ *How did the woman react? (v18)*

▶ *How about Elijah? (v19–21)*

▶ *What did God do and how did the woman's attitude change? (v22–24)*

This widow was not one of God's people — she probably worshipped fake god Baal. But she saw God's power and love and realised who was really in control. And that God's words (through His messenger Elijah) were true.

PRAY ABOUT IT

Thank God that His word is both powerful and true, and that He cares for people, whatever their background.

→ TAKE IT FURTHER

A diversion to Jericho — page 117.

51 Sitting on the fence

Ahab was the most evil of kings. He worshipped Baal, the god of rain. The Lord sent Elijah to speak against him. And to show how useless Baal was, God stopped it raining for three whole years.

👁 **Read 1 Kings 18 v 1–15**

ENGAGE YOUR BRAIN

▷ What did God tell Elijah to do? (v1)

▷ How did Ahab's servant, Obadiah, serve God? (v3–4)

▷ How did Elijah leave him panicking? (v8–14)

▷ And how did Elijah put Obadiah's mind at ease? (v15)

👁 **Read verses 16–29**

▷ How had Ahab caused trouble for Israel? (v18)

▷ What was the Israelites' main problem? (v21)

▷ What amazing challenge did Elijah lay down? (v22–24)

▷ What was Baal's response to all the praying, shouting and self-mutilation? (v29)

God's people had turned away from Him and were following stupid, fake gods. This was a crunch time for them and it was Elijah's job to call them back to God. They were sittin

on the fence (v21) and had to decide who to follow. This test showed how useless any idols or false gods are. The prophets of Baal went crazy; there was blood, sweat and tears; but Baal had no power, so their chants were useless. Tomorrow we'll see what happened next.

SHARE IT

▷ What do your friends trust in or devote themselves to?

▷ How can you show that these things don't match up to God?

PRAY ABOUT IT

Pray for friends who believe in horoscopes or other gods. Pray for friends who devote themseves to something other than God (relationships, work, sport, partying etc). Ask God to shake their faith in wrong things.

➡ **TAKE IT FURTHER**

God stuff on page 117.

52 | Fire proof

God's prophet, Elijah, challenged evil Ahab and the prophets of Baal. Whichever god could set the sacrifice on fire was the true God. So far, Baal's prophets have proved their god can do nothing. Now it's the Lord's turn.

👁 Read 1 Kings 18 v 30–40

▶ *What did Elijah do to make God's fire more impressive? (v33–35)*

▶ *What did Elijah ask God to do? (v36)*

▶ *Why? (v37)*

▶ *What did God do? (v38)*

▶ *How did the people respond? (v39)*

▶ *What happened to the false prophets? (v40)*

God can do anything! Elijah wanted God's people to remember what He was like. To remember that God would forgive His people's disobedience if they turned back to Him. But it would take a sacrifice. And if they continued to follow other gods as Baal's prophets did, they'd be severely punished (v40).

👁 Read verses 41–46

▶ *What did Elijah promise after years of drought? (v41)*

▶ *Did it look rainy? (v43)*

▶ *What two things did God do? (v45–46)*

Once His people's sin had been taken away by sacrifice, God gave rain once more. In some style, too (v45). The Carmel contest showed Baal was no god at all. And it showed the God of Israel had power. And was prepared to forgive His people.

PRAY ABOUT IT

Thank God that He's the one and only. Pray that you and your friends would realise that. And thank God for sending Jesus as the ultimate sacrifice to offer us forgiveness.

→ TAKE IT FURTHER

No *Take it further* today.

53 | On the run

After the big burn out on Carmel, it was now Elijah's turn. To feel burned out. How would God deal with him?

👁 **Read 1 Kings 19 v 1–9**

ENGAGE YOUR BRAIN

▶ What was Jezebel's ridiculous response to God's power? (v1–2)

▶ How did Elijah cope with Jezebel's murderous threats? (v4)

▶ What did God provide for him? (v5–8)

Elijah showed huge courage and trust in God while battling Baal's prophets. But his trust in God evaporated under Jezebel's vicious threats. Yet God picked Elijah up and strengthened him. Elijah travelled many miles to Horeb — the special mountain where God had met Moses.

👁 **Read verses 9–18**

▶ Why had Elijah run away? (v10)

▶ Surprisingly, how did God show Himself to Elijah?

▶ What did He tell Elijah to do? (v15–17)

▶ Yet what was the small sign of hope? (v18)

God spoke in a whisper. He speaks in words, so there's no confusion. To us, that's through the Bible. And He gave Elijah a new task — appointing kings and prophets to carry out a massacre. God's punishment of His people for rejecting Him, worshipping idols and murdering God's prophets.

THE BOTTOM LINE

God will punish those who reject Him. But He'll protect and care for those who serve Him, even when they mess up or run away or have doubts.

PRAY ABOUT IT

Only you know what you need to pray about today.

→ **TAKE IT FURTHER**

Meet Elisha on page 117.

54 : My God is so big

The King of Aram (modern day Syria) was about to wade in on Israel's capital, Samaria. But he underestimated Israel's God. The battle was also a last test for Ahab. Would he change and start serving God?

Read 1 Kings 20 v 1–21

ENGAGE YOUR BRAIN
- What did Ben-H demand? (v2)
- Then what? (v6)
- So what happened? (v9–10)
- What did God promise? (v13)
- What happened? (v19–21)

True to form, God brought victory: with unusual tactics (v19), strange timing (v16) and inexperienced fighters (v15).

Read verses 22–34

- What mistake did the enemy make? (v23)
- How did the two armies compare? (v27)
- Why did God defeat the Arameans this time? (v28)
- Despite God giving him the victory, what did Ahab do? (v34)

Oh dear. Ahab struck a deal with the guy who'd just tried to wipe out God's people in Israel. Idiot! What should he have done?

Read verses 35–43

- Why the harsh-seeming punishment? (v35–36)
- What was God's message for King Ahab? (v42)

Ahab had blown it. God wouldn't give him any more chances. Ahab had brought his own punishment on his head. We learn loads about God in this chapter. His grace is incredible and beyond our understanding. He will punish sin. The Lord is amazingly powerful, can do anything and often uses weak people to achieve His plans. We shouldn't underestimate God as the Arameans did — He's the God of everything, not just "the hills and valleys".

PRAY ABOUT IT

Pray that your view of God wouldn't be too limited and that you'll serve Him wholeheartedly, not compromising when it comes to sin.

→ TAKE IT FURTHER

Go beyond the hills on page 118.

Another vine mess

The Ahab–Jezebel double act sunk to a new low. In the next story, we get cowardice, theft, murder and one of the most grumpy, infantile, self-centred tantrums in history. Oh, and Ahab does something totally out of character.

👁 Read 1 Kings 21 v 1–16

ENGAGE YOUR BRAIN

- ▶ What did Ahab want? (v1–2)
- ▶ What was Naboth's reply? (v3)
- ▶ How did Ahab react? (v4)
- ▶ Who wore the trousers in Ahab's house? (v5–7)
- ▶ What did Ahab allow to happen? (v8–14)

👁 Read verses 17–29

- ▶ What was God's response to their action? (v19)
- ▶ What would happen to Ahab and why? (v20–22)
- ▶ And Jezebel? (v23)
- ▶ How is Ahab's reign summed up? (v25–26)
- ▶ How did God show mercy to Ahab? (v28–29)

Ahab and Jezebel were evil and powerful and could do whatever they wanted. But even kings and queens must bow before God. He's in control, and anyone who rejects His ways will have to answer to God. Yet if people say sorry to God and repent, He will show them mercy.

For Ahab, that meant God would hold back His punishment for a generation. For us, the news is even better. No matter how badly we've treated God, He offers us the chance to say sorry and turn back to Him. If we trust in Jesus' sacrificial death for us, we can be forgiven and start a brand new life with God.

PRAY ABOUT IT

Who needs to make this step and start again? Yourself? A friend? A relative? That girl who really annoys you? Pray that God would show them His incredible grace and mercy and turn their lives around.

THE BOTTOM LINE

Anyone can receive God's grace.

→ TAKE IT FURTHER

A little bit more on page 118.

56 | Ahab's end

What's the difference between a true spokesman of God and a false one? And what's the difference between a good king over God's people and a rubbish one? Well, this chapter has the answers; come and spot the difference.

👁 Read 1 Kings 22 v 1–12

ENGAGE YOUR BRAIN

▷ What did Jehosh and Ahab plan together? (v3–4)
▷ But how was Jehosh different from Ahab? (v5)
▷ Had Ahab changed his attitude to God much? (v8)
▷ What did the 400 prophets claim? (v12)

👁 Read verses 13–28

▷ What did most people want Micaiah to say? (v13)
▷ What was his reply? (v14)
▷ What was God's message to Ahab? (v17)
▷ Why had the other prophets said something else? (v23)
▷ How was Micaiah's message received? (v24, 26–27)

It's not easy telling people the truth. A Christian who wants to be true to the Bible will sometimes have to say stuff people won't like. The message of Jesus often brings out anger and opposition. But God is on our side, helping us share difficult truths.

👁 Read verses 29–40

▷ What precautions did Ahab take? (v30)
▷ But how did God's word come true anyway? (v34–35)
▷ What earlier gory promise also came true? (v38)

We won't always like God's message, but there's no escaping it. God always keeps His promises and we ignore them at our peril. And whatever we do in life, to do it well means obeying God and speaking the truth.

GET ON WITH IT

▷ How can you speak God's truth more and not just say what will please people?
▷ What do you need to change so you're living a good life that serves God?

→ TAKE IT FURTHER

Answers on page 118.

57 | End of part one

Well done! You've reached the end of Kings — Part One. We've seen so much action and excitement. And these two final kings sum up the whole book: some of God's people serving Him, but many rejecting Him.

👁 **Read 1 Kings 22 v 41–50**

ENGAGE YOUR BRAIN

▶ *What was good about King Jehoshaphat? (v43, 46)*

▶ *What wasn't so good during his reign? (v43)*

Like his father — Asa — Jehoshaphat lived God's way and even stopped male prostitution (v43). But he didn't wipe out all the bad stuff that was going on, and he made peace with the evil kings of Israel. We must be careful not to compromise when it comes to sin. If we let a little bit in, it can eventually take over.

👁 **Read verses 51–53**

▶ *How did Ahaziah in Israel compare to Jehoshaphat in Judah?*

▶ *How did God respond to him?*

Ahaziah continued in the way of his ancestors, leading the Israelites into sin and idol worship. You'd think he might have learned from God punishing his dad, Ahab. But no, even though we know the consequences of sin, we're still tempted by it. And so God would punish Ahaziah, his family and his nation. He should have feared God, and so should we.

This may seem a boring way to finish a book. But this isn't the end of the book at all. 2 Kings continues the story, telling us what happened to evil Ahaziah and documenting the amazing things that happend to the prophet Elisha. We'll pick up the story of Judah and Israel next issue.

THINK IT OVER

▶ *What has the book rammed home to you about God?*

▶ *How should it change your attitude to God's words?*

→ **TAKE IT FURTHER**

The final final part of part one can be found on page 118.

58 | 1 Corinthians: Put others first

Back to Paul's letter to the church in Corinth. One of the big messages of the letter is "put others first". And that should be true in both our evangelism and our giving. Pray now that God would speak to you through this letter.

👁 Read 1 Corinthians 9 v 1–6

ENGAGE YOUR BRAIN

▷ *What could Paul have boasted about? (v1–2)*
▷ *What rights could he have claimed? (v4–5)*

Paul was an apostle —someone who had met the risen Jesus and was given the special job of passing on the gospel. He had loads he could boast about. He could have claimed food, drink and money from these people. But he didn't — Paul worked (making tents) so he could afford to go out and tell people about Jesus.

👁 Read verses 7–12

▷ *What point does Paul make in v7–10?*
▷ *Yet had Paul taken payment for his gospel work? (v12)*

👁 Read verses 13–18

▷ *What responsibility do we have for Christians who spread the gospel? (v13–14)*

▷ *Why didn't Paul boast about his work or take payment? (v16–18)*

Jesus sacrificed His life to rescue sinners like us. Paul was telling people about Jesus and made sacrifices too. He wasn't in it for the money or fame — His reward was the joy of sharing the gospel with anyone and everyone. The message of Jesus is free for all. And it's a privilege to tell people about Jesus, not a chore.

SHARE IT

▷ *What stops you telling more people about Jesus?*
▷ *How do you need to change your thinking?*
▷ *And how can you support gospel work?*

PRAY ABOUT IT

Talk to God about anything He's placed on your heart today.

→ TAKE IT FURTHER

Find the reward on page 119.

59 | Run for the prize

More great gospel-spreading tips from Paul. Yesterday he said: Don't demand your "rights" if it gets in the way of spreading the gospel. Now he says: Forget your rights and put other people's preferences first. For the gospel.

👁 **Read 1 Corinthians 9 v 19–23**

ENGAGE YOUR BRAIN

▣ Why did Paul give up a lot of his rights and privileges? (v19)

▣ What did Paul do to spread the message that Jesus saves? (v20–22)

▣ Why? (v23)

Paul knew that to get close to people to share the gospel with them, he had to accept some of their customs. So, when with Jews, Paul would dress rightly, eat kosher food, etc. When with Gentiles ("those not under the law"), he'd eat pork and dress differently, etc. That doesn't mean we should accept or do stuff that's clearly against God's word (getting drunk, sexual sin etc) but it does mean putting others' needs first. That's how important it is to share the gospel.

👁 **Read verses 24–27**

▣ What do believers need to do?

(v24–25)

▣ What's the great reward? (v25)

▣ How did Paul's lifestyle help him with his mission? (v26–27)

SHARE IT

▣ Imagine Paul lived in your area: what are the different groups he would have gone to and how would he have behaved?

▣ Which groups of people should you get involved with more?

PRAY ABOUT IT

Think how you'll apply these principles, following Paul's example. Ask God to give you the same single-minded passion for sharing the truth about Jesus.

➔ **TAKE IT FURTHER**

Prize yourself away to page 119.

60 | Careful, don't fall!

Don't get too smug or comfortable. The Corinthians thought they were doing rather well. Thought they could ease up in their commitment. Unlike Paul. He now shows just how dangerous self-satisfaction can be.

👁 Read 1 Corinthians 10 v 1–5

The Israelites had been led by God (using a cloud and their leader Moses) through the Red Sea, rescuing them from Egypt (v1). God gave them miraculous food and drink to keep them alive and He fed their spiritual needs too (v3–4). Despite all this, they still turned away from God. Paul is saying to Christians: Don't make the same mistake. God sent Jesus to rescue you and He's blessed you so much — don't sit back and take it easy or sin will take over.

👁 Read verses 6–13

ENGAGE YOUR BRAIN

▶ What should we learn from the Israelites? (v6)

▶ What specific sins must we fight?
v7:
v8:
v9:
v10:

▶ What's the big warning? (v12)

▶ What's the double good news in v13?

What happened to the Israelites must serve as warnings for us. We're in danger. Watch out! But there is a way out from each temptation: the moment of choosing whether to give in to it or not.

GET ON WITH IT

▶ What temptations do you face?

▶ What escape route do you need to take?

PRAY ABOUT IT

Thank God for the superb privileges Christians have. Now talk to God about the biggest temptations you face in life.

THE BOTTOM LINE

Don't fall into the temptation trap — take the escape route.

→ TAKE IT FURTHER

Follow the exodus to page 119.

61 Idle idol worship

Idolatry, blood, bread, sacrifices and demon worship. How could all that possibly have any relevance to us in the 21st century? Read on to find out.

👁 Read 1 Corinthians 10v14–22

ENGAGE YOUR BRAIN

- ▶ *What should we do when tempted to put things above God? (v14)*
- ▶ *What do we remember when we take part in communion / the Lord's Supper? (v16)*
- ▶ *How are Christians linked when they eat this meal? (v17)*
- ▶ *Why should these Christians not take part in festivals for idols? (v20–21)*
- ▶ *How does God feel when people worship other gods? (v22)*

Paul mentions three meals: the Lord's Supper, when the Corinthian church met (v15–17); meals after Jerusalem temple sacrifices (v18); and feasts at Corinth's idol temples (v20–21). Paul says that with each meal the person who eats identifies with the people that are meeting and the sacrifices that have been offered. For Christians, it is Jesus' sacrifce on the cross; for Jews, an Old Testament altar sacrifice; for the pagans, a sacrifice to the god of the local temple.

Those idol worshippers don't worship a real God, of course, but demons take advantage of their worship (v20). Don't rob God of the glory He's due. You can't take Him on (v22). And v14 says don't even get near things which you know don't help you honour God.

GET ON WITH IT
- ▶ *What idolatry do you need to run from?*
- ▶ *How will you be involved with your non-Christians friends, yet not influenced by their attitudes?*

PRAY ABOUT IT
Pray that you won't compromise your beliefs, make God jealous or worship anything other than Him.

THE BOTTOM LINE
Run from idol worship.

→ TAKE IT FURTHER
Don't be idle — go to page 119.

Feast on this

"I've been forgiven by God, so I can do whatever I like now, can't I?" "I have to look after number one and not worry what others do — that's their choice." Do you agree or disagree with these statements?

👁 Read 1 Corinthians 10v23–30

ᐅ *How does Paul answer the first statement above? (v23)*

ᐅ *And the second? (v24)*

ᐅ *How should we act when we're with unbelievers?*
  v27:
  v28:

We have freedom, but it would be foolish to use that freedom to do stuff that offends God or stops unbelievers getting closer to God. These verses are tricky, but Paul is doing two things: 1. Encouraging Christians to put others first and realise our actions affect them. 2. Encouraging nervous Christians that it's OK to enjoy the good things in God's world.

👁 Read 10 v 31 – 11 v 1

ᐅ *What are Paul's 3 big principles?*
  v31:
  v32:
  v1:

Christians today aren't worried by sacrificial meat, so let's look at the principles here: Jesus laid down everything — even His life — for others. Paul's doing the same here and so should we. Sometimes there are things a Christian may do that he or she still thinks is not a good thing to do. And sometimes there are things a Christian does that surprise other people.

TALK IT OVER

ᐅ *Are there things you do that other Christians wouldn't do? What does Paul say to you?*

ᐅ *Are you critical of Christians who do things you think are wrong yet the Bible doesn't prohibit them? What would Paul say?*

PRAY ABOUT IT

Read v31–32 again and talk to God about what this means for the way you live.

→ TAKE IT FURTHER

Feast on more words on page 119.

Hair today, gone tomorrow

If you enjoy a little controversy, get ready for this next section. It's all about the differences between men and women, worshipping God and, er, hats. Yes, hats.

👁 **Read 1 Corinthians 11 v 2–16**

ENGAGE YOUR BRAIN

ⓓ *Which verses surprise you?*
ⓓ *Do any offend you?*

These Christians thought there were no differences between men and women (apart from the obvious). Paul says the church must accept God's way of ordering His world (v3). God has put an order to creation where Jesus Christ is the head of the church (all Christians). Within the church, a man (probably "husband") is head of a woman (probably "wife"). Being "head" doesn't mean dictator, but it does mean authority.

Verses 4–7: Back then you could usually tell a man from a woman by their haircut (their clothes were similar). Men usually had shaven heads and women had long hair. Paul says recognise and enjoy the differences. But a woman was to cover her head (v6): maybe so she wouldn't distract men from worship.

Or perhaps to show her willingness to accept her husband's authority.

Verses 6–7: Don't worry: Paul doesn't mean women must wear hats, but that differences in gender are to be celebrated, not rubbed out.

THINK IT OVER

ⓓ *How does Paul say men and women are different, but need each other? In which verses?*
ⓓ *Does he want both men and women to contribute?*
ⓓ *What limits does he give?*
ⓓ *How does society try to blur the differences between men and women?*

PRAY ABOUT IT

If you're confused by any of the issues here, please ask an older Christian. Pray that you would have a right, godly view of gender.

➡ **TAKE IT FURTHER**
Baffling angel stuff on page 120.

64 | Food fight

For you, what makes a good Christian meeting? And what about a bad one? Well, the church in Corinth's meetings were not looking good — arguments, selfishness and drunkenness. I bet that's even worse than your church!

👁 Read 1 Corinthians 11v17–22

ENGAGE YOUR BRAIN

- ▶ What was the problem? (v17–18)
- ▶ What were they each trying to show? (v19)
- ▶ What was wrong with the way they took communion? (v20–21)

When they ate the Lord's Supper together, they were remembering Jesus' death. Yet they didn't treat it with respect — stuffing their faces, getting drunk, arguing, not sharing. This showed their lack of respect for each other as God's people.

👁 Read verses 23–26

- ▶ When Christians eat this meal together, what should they remember? (v24–26)
- ▶ And what should they look forward to? (v26)

Breaking bread was a common meal-time action: Jesus' words give this particular meal far-reaching significance. It was no sad death

of a guru. This was the deliberate, sacrificial death of God's Son, on behalf of self-centred rebels.

👁 Read verses 27–34

- ▶ What's Paul's command? (v28)
- ▶ What's the double warning? (v27, 29)

Don't treat Jesus' death lightly (v27), nor His church ("the body", v29). We should examine how we're getting on with the Christians around us. Otherwise God will discipline us (v32).

GET ON WITH IT

- ▶ If you're a Christian, do you eat this meal with other believers?
- ▶ Why / why not?
- ▶ How will you take it more seriously?
- ▶ What personal action will you take before the next Christian meeting?

➡ TAKE IT FURTHER

Covenant stuff on page 120.

Gift aid

If we're talking "spiritual", those Corinthians thought they were Seriously Super Spiritual. In chapters 12–14, Paul has to explain what it really means to be spiritual. It's a slap in their face. Here's part one.

👁 **Read 1 Corinthians 12 v 1–6**

ENGAGE YOUR BRAIN

▶ *What is Paul's test for true spirituality? (v1–3)*

▶ *What does he say about spiritual gifts? (v4–6)*

These guys thought they knew it all. Paul said they didn't really know what it means to be spiritual (v1). Forget what you learned as unbelievers (v2). What they needed to know now was that anyone who recognises Jesus as King of their lives has the Holy Spirit in them. It's not about having specific gifts. All Christians are spiritual.

There are loads of different spiritual gifts and different ways of serving God. But there's only one God. Christians should be united, working together for God, whatever they're good at.

👁 **Read verses 7–11**

▶ *What do these Christians need to realise? (v7)*

▶ *What does the huge variety of gifts (v8–10) tell us about God?*

We don't know what all these gifts were: some were clearly supernatural, some not. The lesson behind them, though, is not to get so hung up on individual gifts that we ignore the reason God gives them — to build each other up (v7).

GET ON WITH IT

It can be hard working out what gifts God has given us, so... ask Him to help. Ask others. But, more importantly, ask: What can I do to build up other Christians? Then take those opportunities.

PRAY ABOUT IT

And pray for Christians you know to build each other up.

➡ **TAKE IT FURTHER**

Open more gifts on page 120.

66 Body parts

Every Christian is a work of God's Spirit and should use whatever God gives him or her to build up others. That's the way to honour Jesus. That's being spiritual. But some Christians ignore others who have different gifts to them.

Read 1 Corinthians 12v12–20

ENGAGE YOUR BRAIN
▷ How is the church like a human body? (v12–13)
▷ What attitude should we avoid? (v14–16)
▷ Why? (v18–20)

Baptised in v13 isn't talking about being dunked or splashed in water. Here it means the process of becoming a Christian — God's Spirit washing through us, bringing us under Jesus' rule. This happens to all Christians and we all become part of the same body. Everyone has their own role and we shouldn't envy those who are different from us.

Read verses 21–31
▷ What's another attitude we should avoid? (v21)
▷ What's the truth? (v22–25)

Christians need to rely on each other — everyone has an important part to play. God has given Christians a variety of gifts — they're not all the same. Paul says the Corinthians are to desire the "greater gifts": those that communicate God's word to others (see 14 v 1–5).

GET ON WITH IT
▷ Who do you need to think more highly of?
▷ Who do you need to develop a closer relationship with?
▷ Who will you build up this week?

PRAY ABOUT IT
Ask God to give you a healthy attitude towards other Christians. Now pray for specific Christians you know who have some of the gifts/ roles mentioned in v28.

THE BOTTOM LINE
One body, many important parts.

→ TAKE IT FURTHER
Body of evidence on page 120.

67 | Love is...

👁 Read 1 Corinthians 13 v 1–7

ENGAGE YOUR BRAIN

▷ *How can having spiritual gifts without showing love offend people? (v1)*

▷ *What is love like? (v4–7)*

▷ *What's it not like? (v4–6)*

▷ *Which Christians do you find hard to love like this?*

Outrageous. Paul doesn't say that people with these spiritual gifts are unimportant. He says they're nothing (v1–3). About as useful as the gongs in pagan temples. Dramatic acts of self-sacrifice (v3) are pointless if they're done out of self-interest. We must show real, kind, patient, truthful, trusting, hope-filled, persevering love to other believers.

👁 Read verses 8–13

▷ *What is life like now? (v11–12)*

▷ *What will it be like in perfect eternity with God? (v12)*

All of the things we value now will seem insignificant when we experience life in perfection with God. We will know God so much more clearly and it will be awesome. So we should live with our eyes fixed on heaven. And we should show unselfish love as we put others first.

GET ON WITH IT

How does God want you to live? To find out, read v4–7 out loud, replacing "love" and "it" with your name. Go on, try it.

▷ *How will you pray now?*

▷ *What will it mean for you to behave like this with Christians you know?*

▷ *Like who exactly, and how?*

▷ *What will you do the next time you meet them?*

→ TAKE IT FURTHER

Feel the love on page 120.

68 Tongue tied

Paul now focuses on two gifts: tongues (probably a God-given ability to speak another language without learning it) and prophecy (speaking and applying God's truth so it can be understood).

👁 Read 1 Corinthians 14 v 1–12

ENGAGE YOUR BRAIN

▶ What's the difference between tongues and prophecy? (v2–4)

▶ What is the problem if the church meeting is full of people speaking in tongues? (v9–11)

▶ What's Paul's command? (v12)

THINK IT OVER

So when the church meets, its members are to do things which build others up. And not do some out of self-interest.

▶ Do you come to church for what you can get out of it, or for what you can share with others?

👁 Read verses 13–25

▶ Do you think about what you're praying or singing (v15), or thanking God for (v16)?

▶ What's Paul's priority for Christian meetings? (v19)

▶ What does Paul want to happen when an unbeliever walks into a church? (v24–25)

It's important that what we do in church both builds up other Christians and is helpful to non-Christians. We need to make sure we talk clearly about Jesus so unbelievers have every chance of having their lives turned around by God.

PRAY ABOUT IT

Ask God to help you build up other Christians you know. Pray specifically about ones you don't naturally get along with. And pray that what you do in church won't leave non-Christians confused about the truth.

→ TAKE IT FURTHER

A little more on page 121.

69 ¦ Chaos in Corinth ¦

The church in Corinth sounds really confusing! People were speaking in tongues but no one was interpreting it. And they were prophesying, speaking over the top of each other. No one could understand what was being said.

👁 Read 1 Corinthians 14v26–33

ENGAGE YOUR BRAIN

▶ What 3 tips does Paul give for speaking in tongues?
v26:
v27:
v28:

▶ And the principles for prophecy?
v29:
v30:
v31:

▶ And why should there not be chaos in the church? (v33)

👁 Read verses 34–40

▶ What's your reaction to v34–35?

▶ How does Paul sum up his teaching in chapter 14? (v39–40)

These verses about shushing women in church are tricky. It seems that there was a problem with women undermining authority. This church suffered various kinds from chaos and disorder — from everyone speaking in tongues, lots of prophecies babbled at once, and also loud wives asking loud questions. So Paul says: a) speaking in tongues should only happen when it's interpreted; b) prophecy should be given in an orderly way; c) noisy wives should save their questions until they're at home with their husbands. Paul isn't saying women should never talk in church — he's trying to sort out the noisy chaos in the church!

GET ON WITH IT

▶ What do you do that disrupts meetings or makes it harder for others to worship God?

▶ How will you put others first when you're at church?

Ask God to help you do these things.

THE BOTTOM LINE

Church should not be chaotic.
Put others first.

➡ TAKE IT FURTHER

More tongues and prophecy — p121.

83

70 Time for a raise

Oh dear. Some Corinthian Christians had no problems believing that Jesus rose from the dead but they thought that was it. They couldn't believe anyone else would be raised from the dead in the same way in the future.

👁 Read 1 Corinthians 15 v 1–8

ENGAGE YOUR BRAIN

🅳 What was Paul reminding them about? (v1–2)

🅳 What is the gospel? (v3–5)

🅳 Who were the witnesses to Jesus coming back to life? (v5–8)

This is the core of the gospel: Jesus Christ died for our sins, was buried and three days later was raised back to life. We rightly focus on Jesus' death for us, but His resurrection, beating death, is equally important. That's why Paul tells us about all the people who saw the risen Jesus. It's not a fairy tale. It's fact.

👁 Read verses 9–11

Paul saw the risen Jesus (Acts 9 v 1–8) and told the Corinthians about Jesus' resurrection. But any of the other witnesses to the risen Jesus would have told the same story.

THINK IT OVER

"Christian" leaders sometimes appear on TV saying Jesus didn't rise from the dead — "it's a story invented to explain some deep experiences some people had then". Nonsense.

🅳 How would you give them a full answer from 15 v 1–11?

🅳 When you try to explain the gospel to someone, do you include Jesus' resurrection?

PRAY ABOUT IT

Thank God that Jesus was not left dead, but is alive today as our guarantee of salvation.

→ TAKE IT FURTHER

Paul meets Jesus on page 121.

71 Raising expectations

Some of the Christians in Corinth didn't believe that anyone would be raised from the dead. Paul says that resurrection is a vital part of Christianity. So if there's no resurrection then the whole faith falls apart.

◉ Read 1 Corinthians 15v12–19

ENGAGE YOUR BRAIN
If there's no resurrection, what's the logical conclusion...
▷ *About Jesus? (v13, 16)*
▷ *About Christians' faith in Jesus? (v14)*
▷ *About a Christian's relationship with God? (v17)*
▷ *About Christians who are already dead? (v18)*
▷ *About life here and now? (v19)*

◉ Read verses 20–28
▷ *What was Paul convinced about? (v20)*
▷ *What does that mean for all believers? (v22)*
▷ *What hasn't happened yet? (v24–28)*

◉ Read verses 29–34
▷ *If there's no resurrection, what's the logical conclusion about Paul's suffering for the gospel? (v30–32)*

Resurrection is a vital part of the gospel. If Jesus wasn't raised back to life, He hasn't beaten sin and death. But Jesus has been raised back to life — He's conquered Satan and all believers will one day be raised to eternal life with Him. Our sufferings in this life are not a waste of time!

THINK IT OVER
Wrong belief soon leads to wrong attitudes (v33) and wrong behaviour (v34). So Paul gives a strong command (v34).

▷ *Could anyone who looked at your life tell that you believed in the resurrection?*
▷ *What will you do about that?*

PRAY ABOUT IT
Ask God to make you so strong in what you believe about Jesus' resurrection that you behave as courageously as Paul.

→ TAKE IT FURTHER
Baptised for the dead??? Page 121.

72 Body building

Last time, we saw that Jesus' resurrection is the promise of our resurrection. Next we'll see it also points to what our resurrection bodies will be like. Paul tries to describe the indescribable — what it will be like to live forever.

👁 Read 1 Corinthians 15v35-44

ENGAGE YOUR BRAIN

- ▷ How does Paul answer people who think God can't overcome death? (v35–38)
- ▷ What do you think Paul is saying about our new, eternal bodies? (v42–44)

God overcomes death every time a seed sprouts to life (v37–38). So raising the dead is easy for God. Everything God has created has been given the right body for its situation (v38–41). And when Christians are raised to live with God for ever, they'll be given new perfect bodies (v42–44).

👁 Read verses 45–49

We've been made in Adam's likeness but when we're raised to eternal life we'll be made like Jesus ("the last Adam") with new spiritual bodies.

👁 Read verses 50–58

- ▷ What can Christians expect to happen? (v51–52)

- ▷ Why don't we need to fear death? (v54–57)
- ▷ If all this is true, how should Christians live? (v58)

Only God knows when all this will happen. But we have His promise that it will, and that we'll be more like Jesus. Until that day, life can be a hassle, but we know we're on the winning side over death and our own sin (v57). Jesus has already won victory for Christians, so they should live lives that show this — standing firm and giving their all to serve Jesus.

GET ON WITH IT

- ▷ How do you need to change your view of death?
- ▷ And your view of this life?
- ▷ How will you give more of yourself to God's work?

THE BOTTOM LINE

Jesus gives us victory!

→ TAKE IT FURTHER

More on Jesus' return on page 121.

73 | Famous last words

Paul's signing off now, and he has a few
final things to say about money, gospel
work, courage and Christian leaders.

Read 1 Corinthians 16 v 1–4

ENGAGE YOUR BRAIN

▷ What's Paul's tip for giving to
Christian work? (v2)

Yet again, Paul says: Put others first.
Christians should put money aside
(the more you've got, the more you
should share) to give to Christian
work and those in need.

GET ON WITH IT

▷ Do you do that?

▷ How much will you give to
your church and to supporting
Christian workers?

Read verses 5–12

▷ What things shaped Paul's future
plans? (v7, 9)

▷ Why should these guys look after
Timothy? (v10)

Read verses 13–24

▷ What final words of advice does
Paul give?
v13:
v14:

GET ON WITH IT

Write down specific ways you will put
this advice into action.

Be on guard:

Stand firm in the faith:

Show courage and strength:

Do everything in love:

PRAY ABOUT IT

Now spend time asking God to help
you to actually do those things.

→ TAKE IT FURTHER

A tiny bit more... on page 122.

87

TOOLBOX

Repetition repetition

One of the main ambitions of **engage** is to encourage you to dive into God's word and learn how to handle it and understand it more. Each issue, TOOLBOX gives you tips, tools and advice for wrestling with the Bible. This issue, we see how the Bible uses repetition to teach us stuff.

LISTEN UP LISTEN UP

One of the ways a Bible writer can get our attention or make sure we don't miss something important is to say it more than once. Our ears should prick up if we see the same word or phrase ocurring again and again. It's clearly something the author wants us to notice — possibly even the heart of what he's trying to say. Check out this famous part of Isaiah:

Surely he took up our infirmities and carried our sorrows, yet we considered him stricken by God, smitten by him, and afflicted. But he was pierced for our transgressions, he was crushed for our iniquities; the punishment that brought us peace was upon him, and by his wounds we are healed. We all, like sheep, have gone astray, each of us has turned to his own way; and the Lord has laid on him the iniquity of us all.
(Isaiah 53 v 4–6)

The New Testament makes it clear that this was a prophecy about Jesus and His death on the cross (1 Peter 2 v 22–25). Notice the kinds of words that get mentioned over and over: "infirmities", "sorrows", "stricken", "afflicted", "pierced", "crushed", "wounds". Clearly the focus is on Jesus going through something horrific.

But also notice words such as "he", "our", "him", "us", "his", "we" and the constant swapping between them. This shows that Jesus did something for us. He went through all this sorrow and pain in our place. He died for us. He took the punishment for our sins ("iniquity", "transgressions") so that we could go free and be forgiven. This is such an important concept to grasp that the writer forces us to focus on it.

It's not just words and phrases that are repeated in the Bible, but ideas too. So in Mark chapter 15, Mark wants us to understand that Jesus really did die (something Muslims still deny). So he tells us that Jesus "breathed his last" (v37), and that Pilate was "surprised to hear that he was already dead" (v44); so he summoned the centurion to ask "if Jesus had already died" (v44) and then gave His body to Joseph of Arimathea, who put it in a tomb (v46). Without repeating many of the same words, Mark has mentioned the same idea about 6 times. It's as if he's saying: Jesus died; and, by the way, He died; oh and did I tell you that Jesus died?

REPEATED TONE REPEATED TONE

This all sounds very easy. All you have to do is find something the author says a few times and that's the main point of the passage. Sadly, it's not quite as simple as that. Grab a Bible and look at this puzzling passage: Revelation 18 v 15–20.

The important point here is not the distance of the ungodly from Babylon ("far off") or their cry ("Woe! Woe, O great city") or even the time taken for the destruction ("one hour"), even though each of these is repeated. In fact, the most important statement is only made once, in the last sentence. Rather than highlighting a particular truth, the repetition here sets the **tone**. People are shaking their heads, crying out over and over. We're supposed to *feel* that; it's supposed to capture our imaginations. Why envy the world and its wealth and success when it will all end in tears?

So, when reading the Bible, we need to ask ourselves: what idea is being repeated here and why? What tone is the writer setting? What exactly does he want us to understand?

DO IT YOURSELF DO IT YOURSELF

Read Daniel chapter 4

- *What important statement about God is repeated three times?*
- *How does this point to the meaning of the chapter?*
- *When King Neb conquered Jerusalem and took God's people away, it must have seemed as if he was more powerful than God. How does Daniel 4 answer that?*
- *How might our repeated phrase comfort Christians today who are being persecuted for their faith?*

74 | Psalms: New songs

How would you describe your singing in church? So loud and enthusiastic people move away from you? Or a little awkward… slightly half-hearted… with your mind wandering?

👁 **Read Psalm 99 v 1, 4–6**

ENGAGE YOUR BRAIN
- ▶ What's the mood?
- ▶ What words describe how people should sing?

👁 **Read verses 7–9**
- ▶ Who will one day join in? Why? (v7–9)

This is a world created to sing, and humanity is a species created to sing — to sing praises to God. One day, the whole universe will sing God's praises (v9), yet we're called to sing today (v1). But why?

👁 **Read verses 1–3**
- ▶ What motivations are we given to sing like this?
- ▶ Three times in three verses we're told about something God has done — what is it?

If we begin to grasp the incredible way God has rescued us, so that one day we'll join all creation in His perfect world, praising Him… if we just begin to appreciate who God is and what He's done for us… then we'll want to sing and shout His praises. And we'll sing in the way this psalm tells us to: loudly, with joy and jubilation (v4). That means if we don't want to sing joyful praises to God, we haven't understood what it means to be saved by Him.

GET ON WITH IT
- ▶ Do you need to spend some time thinking about how God has saved you from His judgment, for life with Him?
- ▶ Does the way you sing with God's people need to change?

THE BOTTOM LINE
If we appreciate God's salvation, we'll want to sing praises to Him.

➔ **TAKE IT FURTHER**
Sing for your supper on page 122.

75 | Wholly holy

Before you start reading this psalm, describe to yourself in a couple of sentences what God is like:

Read Psalm 99 v 1–5

ENGAGE YOUR BRAIN

- How is God described?
- When people think about God, what should they do?
  v1:
  v3:
  v5:

The psalm summarises God in one word: "holy". It means totally set apart, completely different. We must never reduce God to a kind old man up in the sky — He is a mighty, awesome, nerve-wrecking, holy God.

THINK IT THROUGH

- Is this how you think of God?
- What difference would remembering God is like this make to your daily life?
- To "exalt" someone (v5) means to "lift them up". How do you lift God up with what you say?
- And where you go?
- And how you act?

Read verses 6–9

We move on from what God's like to what God does for His people. Moses, Aaron and Samuel (v6) had helped lead Israel.

- What did God do for His people? (v 6–8)

God was always willing to forgive (v 8). But that didn't mean His people escaped the effects of their sin in this life — God's people are disciplined by Him when we step out of line, so that we step back into line. And God's people still die physically — but wonderfully, because He's forgiven us, we can live eternally.

THE BOTTOM LINE

Respect who God is: rejoice in what God does.

→ TAKE IT FURTHER

Climb the mountain to page 122.

76 | Repeat Repeat Repeat Rep...

A good teacher repeats things, so the class learn and remember what's being taught. In a similar way, we need the message of these psalms to be repeated, so we actually remember it.

👁 Read Psalm 100

ENGAGE YOUR BRAIN

▷ What messages from Psalm 95–99 are picked up here?

▷ What does the psalm writer invite us to do? (v1–2)

▷ What does verse 3 tell us about God's relationship with His people?

▷ Why is that such good news?

▷ What should God's people do? (v4)

▷ Why? (v5)

We need to be reminded regularly about who God is and what He does for us, because we're so good at forgetting all about Him and His love. Whenever we remember and appreciate it, we'll respond in a verse 4 way: we'll praise and thank Him.

David says it's not just a good idea to praise God. It's our duty — as He created us. And it should be our desire, too — as God chose us and looks after us. He's the Good Shepherd.

PRAY ABOUT IT

So right now, take advantage of the fact that this is a short psalm and a short study to praise and thank God in prayer. Use the truths about God in this psalm and Psalm 99 to help you speak to Him.

→ TAKE IT FURTHER

Follow the sheep to page 122.

Repeat Repeat Repeat

77 | I will (will I?)

When two people get married, they make promises. They say: "I do" or "I will". Here, we listen to the "I will"s of a king, making promises to God. This is a psalm written by David, Israel's greatest Old Testament king.

👁 Read Psalm 101

ENGAGE YOUR BRAIN

▶ *What is the king promising to do in his own life? (v1–4)*

▶ *What will he do about those who don't live God's way? (v5, 7–8)*

▶ *What about those who are faithful? (v6)*

David wasn't any old king. He was king of God's people as they lived in God's land. His capital, Jerusalem, was "the city of the LORD" (v 8).

Here's a wonderful picture of a perfect king. But it's a tough standard to live up to! Sometimes, David managed to keep his "I will" promises — sometimes, he failed spectacularly (see *Take it further*).

But there is a king coming who will keep all these "I will"s, as He rules God's people in God's place.

👁 Read Revelation 21 v 5–8

👁 Read Revelation 22 v 1–5

Jesus is the one "seated on the throne" (21 v 5); He is the "Lamb" (22 v 1). We're looking at life under His rule when He returns, and it will be amazing.

▶ *Compare these verses with Psalm 101. How is Jesus the true "I will" King?*

GET ON WITH IT

If you're a Christian, you're heading for a perfect life under a perfect King. Be very excited! And, until you get there, get ready to reign with Him (Rev 22 v 5) by living out Psalm 101 in your life now.

→ TAKE IT FURTHER

Will you turn to page 123?

93

78 | Troubling times

Know what it's like to look at life and despair? The guy who wrote this psalm did.

👁 Read Psalm 102 v 1–11

ENGAGE YOUR BRAIN
▷ How's the writer feeling? (v3–11)

THINK ABOUT IT
▷ When was the last time you felt a bit like this (maybe you do today)?

▷ How do you normally react to this situation?

This guy's despairing about his own life. He's weak (v3–5), suffering (v 8), dying (v11).

👁 Read Psalm 102 v 12–28
▷ What does he remind himself about God? (v12)
▷ And about what God does for His people, "Zion"? (v13, 16)

The psalm writer doesn't seek comfort in who he is, but in who God is. He knows he'll "wither away like grass" (v11) — all humans die. He knows one day all creation will

"perish" too (v26). But he knows God is different — "You remain the same, and your years will never end" (v27).

▷ And what does he know God will do for his family? (v28)

And it gets better — God promises: "Whoever believes in [Jesus] shall not perish but have eternal life" (John 3 v 16). The amazing truth of the Bible is that though we are weak, suffering and dying, through following Jesus we can live forever with our strong, perfect and eternal God.

And that's the truth to hang on to when life hits rock bottom.

THE BOTTOM LINE
In struggles, don't look at life and despair: look at God and rejoice.

→ TAKE IT FURTHER
More trouble on page 123.

79 | Matthew: Follow the leader

As we return to Matthew's Gospel, Jesus is in serious mood. He sets His sights on people who stand on the sidelines criticising and passing comment on others rather than following Him.

Read Matthew 11 v 20–24

ENGAGE YOUR BRAIN

▶ Why is Jesus so angry with Korazin, Bethsaida and Capernaum? (v20)

Tyre and Sidon were notorious, idol-worshipping cities. As for Sodom, well, its wickedness was legendary. In fact, in the Old Testament, God destroyed it with a rain of sulphur!

Read verses 25–30

▶ So if Jesus is unhappy with those who criticise and fail to repent, who is it that will be blessed? (v25–26)

▶ What is Jesus offering? (v28–30)

▶ What must we recognise about ourselves?

▶ What will Jesus give us?

▶ What sort of a master is He?

▶ Why is rest so attractive?

▶ In what way are people weary and burdened in life?

It's been God's choice and plan all along (v26). The way of Jesus isn't within reach of proud, religious know-it-alls; it's only for those prepared to come to God in total dependence (v25). What a great invitation (v28) — people then felt weighed down by all the religious demands placed on them. Jesus offers release from that. And, in the future there will be eternal rest. For now, life won't be easy following Jesus (v29) but it's the best life there can be!

PRAY ABOUT IT

Have you ever accepted Jesus' offer in verses 28–30? Do you need to come back and receive His rest again?

→ TAKE IT FURTHER

The yokes on you — page 123.

80 | Sabbath scandal

All this stuff about resting on the Sabbath seems a bit heavy. Remember that keeping the Sabbath special was one of the Ten Commandments and a big deal to the Jewish leaders. But as usual they've missed the point.

Read Matthew 12 v 1–14

ENGAGE YOUR BRAIN

▶ *What were the disciples doing wrong? (v1–2)*

Technically they were working as they were "harvesting" the grain. I know, talk about being picky — the Pharisees were clearly looking for any excuse to attack Jesus.

▶ *How does Jesus defend the disciples in v3–4?*
▶ *What does He point out in v5?*
▶ *What does He say they've misunderstood? (v7)*
▶ *What two things does He say about Himself? (v6, 8)*

Remember the whole point of God's law in the Old Testament? It revealed God's character and what it would mean for His people to live in perfect relationship with Him. Back in Matthew 5 v 17 Jesus told His disciples He had come to fulfil the law and the prophets.

He is the temple — the place where God meets humanity. He is the Lord of the Sabbath — the one in whom we find rest.

▶ *Is God pleased by picky rule keeping?*
▶ *What sort of heart does God want? (v7)*
▶ *How does v12–14 show Jesus' true character and that of the Pharisees?*

GET ON WITH IT

Do you secretly think that as long as you're doing the right things — reading your Bible, praying, going to church/youth group, not swearing or getting drunk — God will be pleased with you? Stop thinking like that and re-focus your eyes on Jesus.

THE BOTTOM LINE

God wants a relationship, not just rule-keeping.

TAKE IT FURTHER

More scandal on page 123.

81 Devil's advocate

Plotting to kill Jesus is bad enough but the Pharisees go one further now and condemn themselves. Oops.

👁 Read Matthew 12 v 22–37

ENGAGE YOUR BRAIN

▶ *What miracle does Jesus perform in v22?*

▶ *What do the people ask themselves? (v23)*

They're not just asking if Jesus is a descendant of David but if He is THE son of David — the promised King and Messiah.

▶ *Shockingly, what is the Pharisees' verdict? (v24)*

▶ *How does Jesus defend Himself using common sense? (v25–29)*

▶ *What amazing event have they missed? (v28)*

▶ *What is His terrible warning in v30–37?*

Some Christians worry that they have somehow committed this unforgivable sin, but Jesus is quite clear. If you say good is evil and that the work of God is the work of the devil, how on earth can you be saved? You're rejecting the very one who can save you!

So blasphemy against the Spirit is refusing to submit to Jesus and become a Christian. Look again at v32 — even those who speak against Jesus can be forgiven. Remember how on the cross He even prays for those who crucified Him?

PRAY ABOUT IT

Naturally our hearts are wicked. It's only by Jesus' death on the cross and by the Holy Spirit coming to live in us that they can be clean. If you've never asked God to do that for you, do it now — don't delay! And if you have, give great thanks to Him and pray for those who are currently facing God's punishment.

→ TAKE IT FURTHER

Extra stuff on page 124.

82 | Something fishy

Yesterday we read about a great healing, a false accusation and a fierce reply. But the Pharisees hadn't finished with Jesus yet.

⊙ Read Matthew 12 v 38–45

ENGAGE YOUR BRAIN

▣ What do the Pharisees demand? (v38)

▣ What is Jesus' response? (v39)

▣ Why do you think He reacts like this?

▣ What sign does He offer them?

▣ What does Jesus mean by the sign of Jonah? (v40)

▣ What did the men of Nineveh do that these Jewish leaders won't? (v41)

▣ What image does Jesus use to show how bad these unbelieving Pharisees are? (v43–45)

It's hard to process the fact that these Pharisees had Jesus Christ, the Son of God, right there in front of them and yet failed so spectacularly to see who

He was. Or did they? We're not just talking about incomprehension here, but real hostility. Perhaps they did grasp who they were dealing with but didn't want Him as their king. It's a terrible thought.

⊙ Read verses 46–50

▣ What amazing truth does Jesus reveal about those who follow Him? (v46–50)

▣ So what does that mean to YOU?

PRAY ABOUT IT

Thank God now for the amazing privilege of being able to call Him "Father" and of having Jesus as your perfect older brother.

→ TAKE IT FURTHER

A little bit more on page 124.

83 | Hide and seed

A very famous parable today, but it may not be quite what you were expecting...

Read Matthew 13 v 1–17

ENGAGE YOUR BRAIN

▷ *How does Jesus teach the crowd — what style does He use? (v3)*

▷ *Why does He use it? (v10–17)*

▷ *Who is "in" and who is 'out'? (v11)*

▷ *Does verse 15 shock you?*

▷ *Why / why not?*

If you always thought parables were illustrating a moral through an easy-to-understand story then v13 may have come as a bit of a shock. Jesus is using parables so people don't understand what He's talking about. Confused? Well look at v11 and v16. Jesus followers can understand because Jesus opens their ears and helps them to grasp God's truths.

SHARE IT

We cannot convince anyone to follow Jesus. He has to open blind eyes. But that doesn't mean we don't need to share the good news — it just takes the pressure off needing to get a result — that's all down to God!

PRAY ABOUT IT

Ask Jesus to be merciful to your friends and family who aren't following Him, to open their eyes and help them to understand that He is the King.

THE BOTTOM LINE

Only Jesus can open our eyes and help us to see.

→ TAKE IT FURTHER

No hiding — seek out page 124.

84 | Seeds revealed

Like a magic eye picture or invisible ink, the hidden meaning of this parable is now made plain...

👁 **Read Matthew 13 v 1–9, 18–23**

ENGAGE YOUR BRAIN

▶ *Fill in the table below using today's Bible bits.*

Where the seed fell	What it reminds us of	What it means

PRAY IT THROUGH

Ironically, as Jesus told this parable, it was coming true at the same time, some would have listened but not understood, others would have seemed to respond but given up later and still others would have heard, understood and been fruitful. Pray that you would be that last kind of soil and ask God to help you sow the seed of the gospel around you today.

→ **TAKE IT FURTHER**

Soily stuff on page 124.

85 | Weed it and reap

Another parable today. Profound truths but hidden from everyone except Jesus' followers.

👁 Read Matthew 13 v 24–30

ENGAGE YOUR BRAIN

▶ What did the man sow?

▶ What happened to the field?

▶ What were the owner's orders?

👁 Read verses 36–43

▶ What is Jesus doing in the parable? (v37–38)

▶ So what can we say about the world around us now? (v38)

▶ Who is in charge throughout events? (v37, 41)

▶ What happens to the enemy — the devil? (v41–42)

▶ What are we all heading towards? (v39–43)

"He who has ears let him hear". There is a warning here for those who listen to Jesus and want to understand. People's responses will only become fully clear to everyone else when God judges, dividing everyone into two groups. For now, the growth of God's kingdom is mostly hidden. The true size of it will only be seen when Jesus returns.

PRAY ABOUT IT

One judgment. Two outcomes. It's both a terrifying and glorious prospect. Talk to God now about your reactions.

SHARE IT

Ask Jesus to help you share the good news about Him with someone today. Remember He does the sowing — it's all under His control.

THE BOTTOM LINE

There will be no escaping God's day of judgment.

→ TAKE IT FURTHER

More weeding on page 125.

86 Cutting the mustard

Can you think of anything tiny that has a huge influence?
Maybe a microchip or a cell from a killer disease?

Read Matthew 13 v 31–35

ENGAGE YOUR BRAIN

- What is the key thing about the mustard seed? (v32)
- What is the key thing about yeast and what it does? (v33)
- What are we supposed to learn about the kingdom of heaven (living with Jesus as King) from these parables?
- Do you ever feel that your church / youth group is totally powerless, weak and insignificant? How do these parables help shift your perspective?

Here is a man who was born in an obscure village, the child of a peasant woman. He worked in a carpentry shop until He was thirty. Then for three years He was a travelling preacher. He never owned a home, never wrote a book, never had a family, never travelled two hundred miles from the place He was born. He didn't do any of the things that usually accompany greatness. He had no credentials but Himself.

While still a young man, the tide of popular opinion turned against Him. His friends ran away. One of them denied knowing Him. He was turned over to His enemies and was nailed upon a cross between two thieves. While He was dying His executioners gambled for the only piece of property He had – His coat. When He was dead, He was laid in a borrowed grave through the pity of a friend.

Twenty long centuries have come and gone, and today He's the centrepiece of the human race. All the armies that ever marched, all the parliaments that ever sat and all the kings that ever reigned, put together, have not affected the life of people on this earth as powerfully as that one solitary life. (Quote by James Francis.)

PRAY ABOUT IT

Thank God for how His amazing plan was put in place before creation (v35) and how it changed the world.

→ TAKE IT FURTHER

More thoughts on page 125.

87 | True treasure

Three more short and sweet parables to help broaden our understanding of what God's kingdom is like.

👁 **Read Matthew 13 v 44–52**

ENGAGE YOUR BRAIN

▶ *What do the parables in v44–45 tell us about God's kingdom?*

▶ *How does this differ from your attitude to Jesus and living for Him?*

▶ *Would you give up everything to follow Christ? If not, why not?*

PRAY ABOUT IT

The apostle Paul writes: "To live is Christ, to die is gain". Can you honestly say that? Ask God to give you that wholehearted love that treasures Jesus above everything.

GET ON WITH IT

Is there something obvious which you know is standing between you and living all out for Jesus? Non-Christian boyfriend or girlfriend? Making academic or sporting success an idol? Internet porn? Wanting to be in with the cool crowd? Get rid of it!

▶ *Why is it so important to understand the parable in v47–50?*

▶ *What should understanding lead to? (v52)*

The previous parables have all been about what the kingdom of heaven (life with Jesus as King) is like, but this last one is about every teacher who has been instructed by Jesus. The treasures that Jesus has shown us — the treasure of the kingdom — needs to be brought out of the storeroom and put on display.

SHARE IT

How can you display the treasure of the good news about Jesus today?

THE BOTTOM LINE

Christianity isn't just a lifestyle choice — it's life or death.

→ TAKE IT FURTHER

Hunt for the treasure on page 125.

88 | Roots of rejection

Ever get sneered at by people who knew you before you were a Christian? Maybe your friends or parents think it's all a flash in the pan or that you'll grow out of this "religious phase"? Take heart, you're in good company!

👁 Read Matthew 13 v 53–58

ENGAGE YOUR BRAIN

▷ Where does Jesus head to next? (v54)

▷ What sort of a reception does he get? (v54–57)

▷ How does Jesus react? (v57)

▷ What is the verdict on his old neighbours? (v58)

As we look back with the benefit of hindsight, it seems incredible that people had Jesus right there in front of them and yet didn't have faith. But God knew all along that this would happen.

The first chapter of John's Gospel tells us that: *"He was in the world, and though the world was made through him, the world did not recognise him. He came to that which was his own, but his own did not receive him. Yet to all who received him, to those who believed in his name, he gave the right to become children of God"* (John 1 v 10–12).

▷ What great promise had Jesus made in Matthew 12 v 49–50?

PRAY ABOUT IT

It can be really disheartening when the people closest to us are the least interested in Jesus. But take heart, Jesus knows what that feels like. Talk to Him now about it.

THE BOTTOM LINE

When our human families and friends reject us, we have a heavenly Father.

→ TAKE IT FURTHER

Family facts on page 125.

Christianity

89 | Murder in mind

Back in chapter 12 we saw the Pharisees plotting to kill Jesus. In chapter 13 we saw stubborn unbelief, and now we get the first grim example of the opposition that Jesus and His followers will face.

👁 Read Matthew 14 v 1–12

ENGAGE YOUR BRAIN

🅳 Why do you think Herod has this opinion about Jesus? (v2)

🅳 What had happened to John the Baptist? (v3, 10)

🅳 Do you think Herod felt guilty? (v1–2)

This Herod was the son of the child-killer from chapter 2 of Matthew's Gospel, and he was just as sinful and obsessed with his position as his father. As tetrarch (official ruler in the north) he thought he could get away with anything, so he illegally divorced his wife to illegally marry his sister-in-law, and then illegally had John the Baptist beheaded without a trial because he had pointed out that what Herod was doing was wrong. Nice guy. Not.

🅳 Why was John imprisoned? (v3–5)

🅳 Why was he killed? (v6–10)

Herod hated John for pointing out his sin but was too afraid of the people to kill him immediately. Again, when he does eventually kill John, it's because he is worried about what his guests will think about him.

PRAY ABOUT IT

Ask God to help you to fear Him and His opinion of you rather than what other people might say or think.

THE BOTTOM LINE

God's people will face murderous opposition.

→ TAKE IT FURTHER

A little bit more on page 125.

90 Bread role

Ah, the miracle of the picnic lunch.
Think you know all about it? Think again.

 Read Matthew 14 v 13–21

ENGAGE YOUR BRAIN

▶ *Why has Jesus headed for a bit of peace and quiet? (v9–13)*

▶ *Considering all that had recently happened, would you expect Him to welcome a huge crowd?*

▶ *What does this show us about Jesus? (v14)*

▶ *Is the disciples' reaction in v15 understandable?*

▶ *Is Jesus' answer? (v16)*

Clearly the disciples wouldn't have been carrying enough food for 5,000 people, so why does Jesus ask them to feed the crowd? He's testing them — they've seen Jesus do amazing things before; will they turn to Him in faith now?

▶ *Why are the events of v17–21 so amazing? List them:*

▶ *Who is the only one who can create something out of nothing?*

▶ *Who is Jesus?*

PRAY ABOUT IT

Ask Jesus to help you trust Him and turn to Him in every circumstance. Thank Him for His care and compassion for His people.

THE BOTTOM LINE

Jesus cares and Jesus creates.

→ TAKE IT FURTHER

Follow the signposts to page 125.

91 | Focus on Jesus

Another famous miracle today. Before you read it, ask God to help you see it with new eyes. Ask Him to teach you new things.

Read Matthew 14 v 22–36

ENGAGE YOUR BRAIN

▶ *After the mass catering of v13–21 Jesus heads for some time out again. Why? (v22–23)*
▶ *Is the disciples' reaction in v25–26 understandable?*

Well, yes and no. It was certainly out of the ordinary. But think about what they had witnessed Jesus doing only a few hours earlier.

▶ *What does Jesus say to calm them? (v27)*

Jesus isn't just saying: "Hello, it's me". He's saying: "It is I" or more exactly "I am". Ring any bells? This is the great "I AM", the God of Israel speaking.

▶ *Why should Jesus' words help the disciples not to be afraid?*
▶ *What does Peter's experience show us?*
▶ *Should we be trying to copy him?*

The point is not to try and be like Peter, as some people would tell us, but to realise where he goes wrong. Keep looking at Jesus, keep trusting in Him, don't be put off by looking at anything else.

▶ *What does Peter cry out in v30?*
▶ *How quickly does Jesus respond?*
▶ *How do the disciples react? (v33)*

PRAY ABOUT IT

Thank Jesus that we know who He is and that if we ask Him to save us, He will. Thank Him for how much more we can see from this point in history than the disciples understood at that moment in the boat. Pray that He would help us to keep our eyes fixed on Him.

THE BOTTOM LINE

Keep your eyes fixed on Jesus.

→ TAKE IT FURTHER

Final focus on page 125.

TAKE IT FURTHER

If you want a little more at the end of each day's study, this is where you come. The TAKE IT FURTHER sections give you something extra. They look at some of the issues covered in the day's study, pose deeper questions, and point you to the big picture of the whole Bible.

1 KINGS

Ruling passion

1 – SON BLOCK

Read verses 11–27

▶ How would you describe Nathan here?

▶ And Bathsheba?

Nathan the prophet saw that something needed to be done, but he didn't just sit around and complain — he took action. He stirred David up to do something and he saved Bathsheba and Solomon from almost certain death.

▶ Are there any situations where you need to intervene and do the right thing?

2 – FATHER'S ORDERS

Read verses 5–8 again

Joab murdered Abner (2 Sam 3 v 27) and Amasa (2 Sam 20 v 8–10) in peacetime. Hmmm, not a nice bloke. Shimei cursed David (2 Sam 16 v 5–14, 19 v 16–23). Cursing God's chosen king earned the death penalty. Why didn't David kill these guys himself? We don't know; maybe he should have. Barzillai (v7) had helped David and his people out when they were on the run, so Sololomon would look after

Barzillai's family in the future. What goes around, comes around.

3 – ENEMY ELIMINATION

Read Matthew 13 v 41–43

▶ What's the terrifying news for God's enemies?

▶ What will be the amazing outcome for believers ("the righteous")?

4 – WISE CHOICE

Read verses 1–2

This marriage (v1) was the start of Solomon's spiritual downfall (wait for chapter 11). Think why it's a disaster.

"High places": see an OK use of one in 1 Samuel 9. But also see God's instructions in **Deuteronomy 7 v 5, 12 v 2–3**.

▶ What were God's people to do about the religions they would encounter in Canaan?

▶ What would happen if they failed to take this action?

5 – LET THERE BE LISTS

Read verses 20–25

This is a great chapter for God's people. The Lord fulfilled so many of His promises made to Abraham, Jacob, David and all of His people. Check them out, it's impressive stuff:

Read Genesis 22 v 15-18 and then 1 Kings 4 v 20.
Check out Genesis 15 v 18–21 followed by 1 Kings 4 v 21, 24.
And finally 2 Samuel 7 v 10–11 with 1 Kings 4 v 24–25.

6 – GRAND DESIGNS
Read 1 Kings 7 v 13–51
You may wonder why you should care how many pomegranates are on that pillar or why we need to know about all that bronze and gold stuff. But the writer of 1 Kings doesn't find it tedious. He loves it! He's suggesting that intricate, careful, detailed beauty is fitting for God. After all look at all the intricate, beautiful things He created. Nothing can be too good or too lavish for our amazing God. We must never offer Him second best. We don't build expensive buildings to praise God, but we should lavish with our time, efforts and worship devoted to God.

7 – PARK THE ARK
Read verses 6–7 again
The cherubim were carved wooden creatures each about 5m high, placed over the ark. They were regarded as the visible footstool of God's invisible throne.
Check out 2 Kings 19 v 15 and Psalm 99 v 1–3

8 – I'D LIKE TO THANK...
Read verses 39, 58, 61
▶ *What was at the heart of the human problem?*
Now read Hebrews 8 v 10–12
▶ *What's so great about the new covenant that Jesus brought?*
▶ *How can you let these awesome truths truly impact your life?*

10 – ROYAL VISIT
Read verse 1 again
Sheba was probably in Arabia (near the Red Sea). Her questions might have been about God but there was probably a lot of trade and business talk going on too (v10, 13). But she did recognise that God was behind Sol's success (v9).

Now read Matthew 12 v 42
The queen of Sheba was not an Israelite yet she heard Sol's words, saw his wisdom and realised it was from God. In Jesus' time, the Jewish people saw and heard even more impressive things — Jesus' teaching and miracles — yet many of them refused to believe He was from God. Don't be as foolish. Don't read all about Jesus and His life-transforming words and then fail to believe them or turn to Him in repentance.

11 – FATAL ATTRACTION
Catch God's warnings about inter-marrying with those who weren't members of God's people: **Deuteronomy 7 v 1–4), Exodus 34 v 16.**
▶ *Is there any warning in this*

for you about your friendships, relationships, people you mix with?

Here are Sol's 6 steps to disaster:

1. He allows himself to be led by his feelings (v1).
2. He ignores God's specific commands (v2)...
3. ...repeatedly (v3).
4. He gives in to peer pressure (v3).
5. He finds his loyalties are divided (v4).
6. He ends up doing things which make God angry and bring His punishment (v5-9).

▶ *Are you slipping down a slope from 1 to 6? In what ways?*

▶ *What counter-action will you take to return to pleasing God?*

12 – THE BIG SPLIT
Read verse 15 again

Whatever happens in life, however good or bad things are, we must remember that God is always in control. We often won't understand His plans. Our role is to obey Him, live for Him and watch His perfect plans unfold, however baffling they seem to us at the time.

1 CORINTHIANS
God, the bad & the ugly

13 – INTRODUCING...
Read verse 2 again

Notice that the church in Corinth isn't called just part of the church. In the Bible,

the church is both something far-reaching (every Christian who's ever lived and is alive today, around the throne in heaven) and local (that bunch who meet in town). The Bible's also realistic. See v4–9 here: the church is God's, yet it's riddled with problems (see v10–17), because it's full of people like you and me who mess it up.

▶ *How does this double truth help you as you get involved in church?*

14 – LONG DIVISION
Read verses 4–17 all together

▶ *Where does the idea of putting others first appear in these verses?*

Now pray about areas of your life where you would like to be more holy. And pray for Christians who you know are in disagreement — and any you disagree with, too.

15 – FOOLISH WISDOM

▶ *Can you explain why Jesus was crucified?*

▶ *Why did He have to be crucified for us to be put right with Him?*

▶ *What other Bible truths do we need to mention if we're to explain "Christ crucified" properly?*

▶ *Can you find other verses to help you do that?*

▶ *Are you ever tempted to make the Christian life sound more glamorous than it is, to win a friend for Christ?*

▶ *Do you ever feel inadequate as a Christian?*

▶ *What do you think God would say to you from today's verses?*

16 – SPIRIT OF WISDOM
Read verse 7 again
There's no plan B that swung into operation when humans rebelled against God (Genesis 3). God wasn't surprised; He'd planned Jesus' rescue mission before He even created the world!

▶ *What does this tell us about God?*
▶ *What other big questions do you have after today's section?*
Read **James 1 v 5** before talking to God.

17 – BUILDING BLOCKED
Read verses 1–4
In all the time since Paul left them, the Corinthians had not become more mature.
▶ *What does it take to grow in maturity as a Christian? (See Ephesians 4 v 11–16)*

Read 1 Corinthians 3 v 18–23
The world's "wisdom" is foolishness. And Christians will be thought of as idiots by people around them.
▶ *What aspects of Christian truth are hardest to stand up for?*
Christians can be easily swayed into thinking like everyone else.
▶ *What are the most obvious ways we do that today?*

18 – SCUM OF THE EARTH
Read verses 4–5 again
Paul aimed to keep his conscience clear by living the best he could for Jesus. But he realised that it's still the cross of Christ that puts him right with God, not good

behaviour. If we become critical of our leaders (like the Corinthians were of Paul), we're trying to do God's work for Him.

▶ *Are you critical of leaders in your church?*
If you've got good leaders, thank God and don't assume you deserve them.

19 – USE YOUR LOAF
▶ *If you discovered that a Christian friend was regularly sleeping with his girlfriend, how do you think Paul would want you to think and act?*
Pray that you won't be judgmental (v12), and that you won't let God's standards slip. See the dangers in **Matthew 7 v 1–5**.

20 – COURT ORDER
Read verse 3 again, and then Daniel 7 v 27, Luke 22 v 29–30 and Revelation 20 v 4.
▶ *What perspective should this give us on the small disputes in life?*

21 – GOD'S BODY
▶ *Exactly how will you "flee sexual immorality"?*
▶ *Ever been tempted to have sex outside marriage? How would you have justified it to yourself?*
▶ *How would Paul reply?*
▶ *Ever speak or act as if God's only interested in your soul and not what you do with your body?*

Read Genesis 2 v 22–24   >>>>

Casual sex is out. That deep uniting between two people was designed by God to give us an insight into His love for us, and how closely we're united to Jesus (Ephesians 5 v 28–33).

For more on our eternal bodies being transformed, check out **1 Corinthians 15 v 42–44, 51–52**.

22 – GOD, SEX AND MARRIAGE
Verses 1–7 are God's guidelines for sex within marriage. Contrary to popular belief, God says: Go for it! And enjoy! Often!
- ▶ *Have you understood God's view of sex correctly?*
- ▶ *Which of these instructions (v2–5) surprises you? Why?*

Christians are supposed to be different from our culture (see Romans 12 v 1–2).
- ▶ *What does Paul say about sex, marriage and being single which is different from the way a) your parents b) your non-Christian friends c) TV and magazines think?*

23 – SINGLE MINDED
Read Genesis 2 v 18–25 and Ephesians 5 v 31–32
Marriage is a great gift from God which teaches us about Christ's love for us. Christians are "married" / joined to Jesus in a marriage that lasts for ever.

Now read Matthew 22 v 30 and Revelation 19 v 7 & 21 v 2
- ▶ *How does this put human marriages in a new light?*

24 – MARRIAGE PROPOSAL
Single? Think how to use your time, money and extra freedom to serve Jesus and others the best you can. Go for it.

Ever resent the fact you can't have sex outside marriage? Or that you might not marry? Talk to God about it. And maybe an older Christian too.

With sex stuff, temptations are big. Feeling guilty? Then trust God's deep forgiveness, through Jesus' death.
Read 1 John 1 v 7–9

25 – FOOD FIGHT
Read verse 1 again
- ▶ *Why is knowledge without love dangerous?*
- ▶ *How does this apply to you in relation to other Christians and to non-Christian friends?*
- ▶ *Are you concerned about a Christian friend's behaviour?*
- ▶ *So how should YOU behave?*
- ▶ *Who irritates you most? Ask God to help you build them up.*

Read Romans 14 v 1 to 15 v 2

SONG OF SONGS
God, sex and wow

26 – SNOG OF SNOGS

Read verses 5–8 again

She has a low opinion of her own looks. Being tanned was not considered so attractive back then, and she wants a makeover (her "vineyard" = her own body). Yet her friends saw her beauty (v8). And God sees our true beauty too, whatever we look like or whatever other people say. Value God's opinion above all, remember He loves you, and try to live a life that's beautiful to Him.

27 – LONG OF LONGINGS

Advice to those who might get married one day (or those who already are): remember to:

a) praise each other. And keep doing so. It's possible to ignore the blemishes (we *all* go wrinkly and saggy), banish the irritations and concentrate on telling your husband/wife what's great about them.

b) take time together. Look at these two (2 v 10, 13, 17) Build your relationship properly. Sex without that is spoiled.

28 – SONG OF SEX

Read Matthew 5 v 27–30

Adultery in the head is the same as adultery in the bed. So, be ruthless in your drive to be holy. If all this talk of sex is sending you into unhelpful, lustful thinking, then quit reading Song of Songs and move on to the next section. Ask God for self-control and a desire to please Him.

Remember 2 v 7 and 3 v 5?

29 – SONG OF FRUSTRATION

Read Song of Songs 5 v 4–5

Amazingly, he doesn't get angry or sulk even though he's very disappointed that she's turned him down. Instead, he covers the door handle with myrrh (a sticky, perfumey substance) as a sign of his continued fragrant love for her (myrrh gets mentioned loads in this song). She's so happy when she discovers it as it drips down over her hand. Thoughtfulness is key in relationships, even when you're frustrated and feeling down.

▶ *What can you do to show someone you've forgiven them or that you appreciate them?*

30 – SONG OF PASSION

Read Song of Songs 6 v 11–12

It's not entirely obvious what's going on here, but it seems to be a picture of reconciliation — they're back together again and all is good.

Read Ephesians 5 v 1–7

▶ *What are we to do, and why? (v1–2)*
▶ *What specific things does Paul say we need to kick out? (v3–4)*
▶ *What's the incentive for right living in v5–6?*
▶ *What do you need to start or stop doing?*

We're God's children and so should imitate Him in the way we live. Remembering Jesus giving up His life for us should motivate us to live His way. Paul homes in on sexual sin. He says there's no place in a Christian's life for greed or impurity, expecially sexually. And that includes dirty jokes (v4). We should thank God for the gift of sex; not mock it or abuse it. In fact, we should stay away from people who do (v7).

31 – SONG OF CELEBRATION

Throughout the Old Testament, God's relationship with His people is described in marriage terms (Hosea chapters 1–3, Jeremiah 2 v 2 and 3 v 1). In the New Testament, the church is Christ's bride, which one day will be "married" to Him and live with Him for ever (Revelation 19 v 7–9).

Not in a relationship? Feel there's no hope? Despairing of never getting married? Well, there's no quick fix, but ask God to help you. Singleness and marriage are both good. Both part of God's plan. Trust His goodness — He has our best interests at heart.

PSALMS

32 – A MASSAH-VE PROBLEM

The New Testament book of Hebrews picks up the warning of Psalm 95 and applies it to Christians.

Read Hebrews 3 v 12 – 4 v 3
- *What the people who Moses led out of Egypt heard was of no value to them (4 v 2). Why not?*

- *Instead of hardening our hearts to God's word, what should we do? (3 v 14)*
- *How can we stop ourselves from being deceived? (v13)*

We need each other! It's your responsibility to help your Christian friends keep holding on to Christ. Verse 13 tells us to do that "daily" — who could you speak to or text or email to encourage them today?

33 – I'M SO EXCITED...

Psalm 96 v 5 reminds us that anything anyone worships apart from the Creator God of the Bible is an idol.

Read Isaiah 44 v 6–22
- *What does God say about Himself? (v6–8)*
- *What does He say about idols and people who worship them (v9–20)?*
- *What are the idols you find easy to love more than God?*

Always remember: when we realise we've treated something else as God, God always says: "Return to me, for I have redeemed [freed] you" (v22).

34 – TERRIFYING OR TERRIFIC?

The writer of Hebrews loved the psalms! In chapter 12 we see more of the imagery used in Psalm 97. The writer's comparing the terror we deserve to feel before God with the joy we can feel about knowing God now that Jesus has died for us. He pictures it as two different "mountains".
Read Hebrews 12 v 18–24

MATTHEW
Follow the leader

35 – HEALING POWER

Check out the rest of the passage
Matthew quotes in v17: **Isaiah 53 v 1–12.**

▶ *What is our greatest need? (v5)*
▶ *How does Jesus heal us?*
▶ *Where was this prophecy ultimately fulfilled?*

36 – NO COMPROMISE

Read Matthew 6 v 24, 31–34

▶ *What had Jesus said about divided loyalties?*
▶ *What else can you add to the list of things that get in the way of following Jesus whole-heartedly?*
▶ *What do you need to do about them?*

37 – STORMING STUFF

Jesus' miracles don't just show us His power, although they do. They don't just give us a clue to His identity, although they do that too. They also point to the reality of His coming kingdom, where there will be no more sickness, death, evil or chaos, like storms and tsunamis. Get a taste for that coming kingdom now, by reading **Revelation chapters 21 & 22.**

38 – PIGGING OUT

It has been said that Christians can make the mistake of taking the devil too seriously or not seriously enough! For an imaginative way of looking at the issue, check out "The Screwtape Letters" by C.S. Lewis. It's a book but there's also a great audio version you could download online.

39 – POWER POINT

Look again at verse 2

It's shocking, isn't it? This man was paralysed — think for a minute about what that is like now and what it would have been like in Jesus' day. He's not just got a bad knee that needs a bandage. But Jesus thinks his spiritual state is even worse...

▶ *Do you think of sin as a life-threatening disease? Should you?*
Pray about it now.

40 – DOCTOR AND BRIDEGROOM

The picture Jesus gives us of Him as the bridegroom is one of the best images in the Bible. Ever been to a good wedding? Well, check out **Revelation 19 v 6–8 and Revelation 21 v 1–4**. We will have a front row seat; in fact, we will be the bride!

41 – HEALING WORDS

Does God do miracles now? Well, of course He *can*. But don't mis-read Matthew: these miracles were pointers to Jesus' identity, not models for our expectations today. But hang on...

Doesn't God do miracles today? Doesn't He turn hard, self-centred individuals into people being re-made like Jesus? Is it true that God can't change human nature? Well, God can: look at lives you've seen Him change — that's a miracle.

42 – MISSION POSSIBLE

To get a deeper understanding of what it means for Jesus to be our Shepherd, look up the following verses and tell God your response.

Numbers 27 v 15–17
2 Samuel 5 v 1–3
Psalm 23
Ezekiel 34 v 1–15

43 – CHRISTIANS IN CONFLICT

Spend some time praying for Christians in other countries who face persecution, imprisonment, torture and death for following Jesus. Ask God to help them to stand firm and not be afraid of men but keep fearing God. Try websites like www.opendoorsuk.org or www. barnabasfund.org

44 – FAITH FIGHT

Read verse 34 again

How could nice, inoffensive Jesus say that (v34)? Wasn't He all about peace? Well, yes, Jesus did come back to bring peace, just as the Messiah was predicted to (Isaiah 9 v 6–7, Zechariah 9 v 9–10). That peace (a restored relationship with God) has begun, but has not yet been completed. So, for now, following the Prince of Peace brings conflict and division.

It's been said that home can be the hardest place to be a Christian.

- *Have you, or your friends, experienced that? In what ways?*

- *How will you stand for Jesus in your home and among your friends?*
- *And how can you be a peacemaker?*

45 – IDENTITY PARADE

Read verse 6 again

Jesus knew people would take offence at Him. After all, He didn't conform to their ideas in what He said or did.

- *In this verse, how does Jesus encourage people to trust Him?*

Now read verse 11

John's been the greatest up to this time — he understood who Jesus is. But any humble Christian since John is greater — we've understood more because we live after Jesus' death and resurrection.

The people of Israel were not willing to accept either John (v14) or Jesus. The response Jesus got from the religious leaders was a sulky refusal to participate (v17), and a grumpy, self-centred criticism about both John and Jesus (v18). Jesus, like John, was being misunderstood and rejected. But God's way of doing things would be proved right (v19). Pray that you'll respond to Jesus rightly, and that you'll never tire of understanding who Jesus is and learning more about Him.

1 KINGS

47 – THE NAME GAME
**Read verses 15–16 again
and then 2 Kings 17 v 22–23**
These things happened as God said
they would.
- *Do you believe that God's words
  about the future (eg: Jesus' return,
  His judgment, heaven and hell) will
  come true?*
- *Why should we?*

48 – A TALE OF TWO KINGS
Look verses 3–4 again
If Abijah followed his father's evil ways,
why didn't God destroy the kingdom in
Judah? Well, God had promised King
David that the kingdom would continue.
Judah wasn't destroyed because of David's
faithfulness to God (he wasn't perfect at
all, but he never turned away from God).
But more importantly, God was faitful to
His covenant promises to David. And from
David's family would come the greatest
King of all — King Jesus. That's why this
kingdom wasn't wiped out.

49 – BAD, BAD, BAD, BAD, BAD
Read 1 Kings 15 v 28–30
This all seems so horrible and godless. But
God *is* there. His word and His promises
are there. All of Baasha's bloodshed took
place "according to the word of the Lord"
(v29). Many times in the Old Testament,
God uses evil men to punish other evil
men. But if those evil men God uses don't
turn to Him, then they'll be punished too

(16 v 2–3). Evil may seem all-powerful but
nothing is more powerful than God. The
Lord is always in charge. Evil can't win.

50 – AHAB VS ELIJAH
**Read Joshua 6 v 26
and then 1 Kings 16 v 34**
In the middle of Ahab's story, this verse
seems very random. But it shows the kind
of bad stuff that was going on during
Ahab's reign. After God helped Joshua to
destroy the city of Jericho, Joshua cursed
anyone who attempted to rebuild it. And
here was the sad outcome.

51 – SITTING ON THE FENCE
**Read verses 27–29
and then Psalm 121 v 1–8**
- *How is God different from all other
  "gods"?*
- *Where can we turn for help? (v1–2)*
- *What does God do for His people?
  (v5)*

53 – ON THE RUN
Read verses 19–21
- *What was Elisha doing when Elijah
  found him? (v19)*
- *How did he make a clean break with
  his farming life? (v21)*

Elisha was a farmer, yet God suddenly
called him to follow Elijah and train
to be God's messenger. Don't get too
comfortable in life. We never know
when God will call us to something or
somewhere new. And when He does, we
must respond positively, as Elisha

117

did. And serving God isn't always pretty or filled with glory, fame or respect. Elisha's mission started out with him ploughing the fields and then following Elijah as his personal servant, and later he was called to get rid of God's enemies (v16). Serving God won't always win us lots of friends, but we must go for it wholeheartedly, as Elisha did. Sometimes we just have to get up and serve God.

54 – MY GOD IS SO BIG
Read verses 23–25 and 28

We can easily make the same mistake as the Arameans — assuming that God is only interested in certain things and certain parts of our life. We put Him in our own boxes and hold back parts of our lives from Him. But the Lord is God of EVERYTHING and so is involved in every aspect of life, and we need to let Him be Lord of our whole lives. Nothing is too big or small for God. And we must never think that we (or other people) are too young, old, uneducated, wealthy, poor, wild, sinful etc to be used by God. He's the God of everything.

55 – ANOTHER VINE MESS
Read verses 27–29 again

Amazingly, Ahab listened to God's words for once and they deeply affected Him. Ahab's response caused God to show mercy to this evil king, despite all he'd done. OK, so Ahab didn't turn fully to God and so God didn't forgive him. But He did show Ahab mercy. God doesn't want to punish us, but He can't let us rebel against Him or let sin go unpunished. He longs for us to turn back to Him in repentance so He can forgive us and restore our relationship with Him.

56 – AHAB'S END

Back to our original questions: What's the difference between true and false prophets? Well, false prophets aimed to please Ahab rather than speak the truth (v6, 14).

And what's the difference between a good king and a bad one? Ahab refused to submit to the authority of God's word (v8, 18). But Jehoshaphat obeyed God (v5).

Someone once said: *"It's a common human reaction to try to silence the word of God when it decrees judgment."*

▶ *When have you seen this to be true?*
▶ *What's your general attitude to God's words — the Bible?*
▶ *Have you faced up to the Bible's words on God's judgment?*
▶ *When the Bible challenges you hard, do you fight it, try to pretend it's not aimed at you, or recognise God's authority and do something?*

57 – END OF PART ONE

1 Kings seems to end with a lot of loose ends that still need to be tied up. But look out for Engage 15 on 2 Kings. It picks up the story of:
the prophets Elijah and Elisha;
God's judgment on Ahab's family;
God's punishment of Ahaziah;

the exile and abandoning by God of Israel;
God's protection of His true people;
And more! Now spend time thanking God
for 1 Kings and all it has taught you.

1 CORINTHIANS

58 – PUT OTHERS FIRST

Paul's defence was directed at those who
questioned his authority as an apostle.
Paul uses himself as an example, not to
boast, but to illustrate how the gospel
must affect Christians' priorities, and their
letting go of "rights".

- *What do you look for as your reward
  in this life?*
- *What should it be? (v18)*

59 – RUN FOR THE PRIZE

Read verse 22 again

"All things to all men" doesn't mean:
a) Paul stops behaving like a Christian in
some situations; b) Paul tries to be popular
with every group; c) he pretends to be
something he's not.

It means he adapts his method (but
not his message) to present the gospel
clearly, as he mixes with people in their
own situations. It's not easy to meet
non-Christians on their own terms. Ask
God to forgive you for looking down on
others, and ask Him to give you the same
commitment and discipline as Paul.

60 – CAREFUL, DON'T FALL!

Here are the Old Testament incidents Paul
was talking about:
the cloud – **Exodus 13 v 17–22**
the sea – **Exodus 14 v 21–22**
the food – **Exodus 16 v 1–35**
the rock – **Exodus 17 v 1–7**
the scattering – **Numbers 14 v 26–38**
the idol worship – **Exodus 32 v 1–8**
the immorality – **Numbers 25 v 1–9**
the testing – **Numbers 21 v 4–7**.

61 – IDLE IDOL WORSHIP

Worshipping anything other than God was
a constant problem throughout the Old
Testament, with dire results. Check out…
Genesis 3
Exodus 20 v 2–3
Deuteronomy 4 v 15–24
God's concern is that He is the only God
and the only one to be worshipped.
That's what Paul means when he talks
of God's "jealousy".

- *What pulls Christians away into
  worshipping other "gods"?*
- *What precautions can you take so
  it doesn't happen to you?*

62 – FEAST ON THIS

Confused by today's reading? Relax, and
ask yourself:

- *Does your behaviour help or hinder
  other Christians?*
- *Can you think of specific recent
  examples for yourself?*
- *Does your behaviour help or hinder
  non-Christians to come to know Jesus*

for themselves?
- *How might this make you pray today?*
- *Does your behaviour match what Jesus would have done?*
- *How will you use actions/opportunites/ words to honour God?*

Freedom! Jesus' death won us the privilege of not needing to keep Old Testament laws. But it doesn't mean we're free to do what we like with no consequences. Paul is clear about this in the letter of Galatians. Check out:
Galatians 3 v 26 – 4 v 7
Galatians 5 v 1, 13–26

63 – HAIR TODAY, GONE TOMORROW
Read verses 8–10
More helpful loads of debate as to what v10 means. "Because of the angels" might mean angels are worried at the Corinthians' disobedience, or that angels were judged by God for not keeping their created place (2 Peter 2 v 4). "Having a sign of authority" may mean: when a woman prays or prophesies (applies God's word to a particular situation) she must acknowledge she's under authority.

64 – FOOD FIGHT
Read verse 25 again
God made a covenant agreement with the people of Israel, saying: I'll be your God, to lead you. And you must live my way. As we all know, they (like us) didn't keep their side of the deal. But in Jesus, God made a new covenant, saying: I'll rescue you from judgment because of

Jesus' death. You must trust Him and live my way.

65 – GIFT AID
Read Ephesians 4 v 11–16,
Romans 12 v 6–8
and 1 Peter 4 v 8–11
- *What leaps out at you from these gift lists?*
- *What do you contribute to your church?*
- *Do you mostly give or take?*
- *How should the church show unity and diversity?*
- *What can you do that will use what God has given you to bring people together rather than push them apart?*

66 – BODY PARTS
To accomplish His purpose on earth, Jesus had a body. And still does — His body is the church! The Bible says the church is both local (your hometown church) and universal (all Christians are part of the same body).
- *What would your church be like if everyone was like you?*
- *Do you sometimes feel you don't fit in to your local church?*
- *What would Paul advise you to do?*

67 – LOVE IS...
Read verse 13 again
Faith, hope and love often get mentioned in the New Testament as things that sum up a Christian's character. And they should. But why is love here called the greatest? Well, in eternity we'll no longer

need hope or faith. But love is forever. So these Christians, big on spiritual gifts but not on love, must get this sorted.

- ▶ How does Paul want to change their attitude?
- ▶ What things do you value more highly than love for God and other people?
- ▶ How are you going to change?

God's preparing us now for eternity. Ask God to give you a generous, loving heart to make you ready for your eternal home.

68 – TONGUE TIED

Some people seem to find it helpful to talk to God in tongues, but you're not more spiritual if you do that (or anything else). Just use the abilities God has given you. Use them to build up others.

- ▶ How will you build up a Christian you don't know very well?

69 – CHAOS IN CORINTH

Paul's 3 tips for handling speaking in tongues:

1. Don't let things go on and on (v27)
2. Make sure it's all explained (v27)
3. If there's a danger of confusion, don't use your gift (v28 suggests speaking in tongues isn't uncontrollable).

3 principles for prophecy:

1. Don't let things go on and on (v29)
2. Make sure it's all examined (v29)
3. Don't dominate the meeting (v30).

70 – TIME FOR A RAISE
Read Acts 9 v 1–19

- ▶ How would you sum up Paul's attitude towards Christianity (The Way)? (v1–2)
- ▶ How does Jesus describe Paul's behaviour? (v4–5)
- ▶ What's so amazing about Ananias' first words to Saul, considering Saul's past?

The good news about Jesus turns enemies into brothers, makes the blind see and transforms persecutors into believers!

71 – RAISING EXPECTATIONS
Read verse 29

Paul doesn't tell us exactly what being "baptised for the dead" means. It was clearly something the church in Corinth was doing, and it was wrong. Some Bible experts think that some Christians in the area had died (possibly killed for their faith) before they'd had the chance to be baptised. So Christians who were still alive were being baptised again on their behalf. Whatever it was, it wasn't something Paul (or the rest of the Bible) says we should do.

72 – BODY BUILDING
Read 2 Peter 3 v 8–16

- ▶ How does Peter explain the delay in Jesus' return? (v8–9)
- ▶ What does that tell us about God? (v9)
- ▶ How is the day of Jesus' return described? (v10)
- ▶ So how should we live now? (v11–12)
- ▶ What should be our attitude towards

heaven? (v13)

▶ How can you apply v14 to your life?

Talk to God about anything that He's put on your mind and heart today.

73 – FAMOUS LAST WORDS

All the people Paul mentions (v10, 12, 15, 17) are colleagues of his who he'll use to keep a close and loving watch on the church in Corinth, while he stays in Ephesus (v8–9). Paul thinks his ongoing contact with the Corinthians is vital.

Read verses 15–16 again

▶ Why must these guys submit to (obey) Stephanas and friends?

▶ What does that tell us about Christian leadership?

▶ So what sort of people should be Christian leaders?

▶ How does that differ from society's view of leadership?

PSALMS

74 – NEW SONGS

Read Romans 3 v 21–26

▶ What has been "made known"? (v21)

▶ How do people get this righteousness, this "being right with God-ness"? (v22)

It's at the cross that God's righteousness — the way He makes people right with Him — is most clearly revealed. Remembering what Jesus has done for

you on the cross, why not re-read Psalm 98 and shout for joy all over again?!

75 – WHOLLY HOLY

Verse 9 tells us to "worship [God] at his holy mountain" — that is, the mountain His temple in Jerusalem sits on.

Read John 2 v 19–22

▶ What does Jesus say about the temple? (v19)

▶ What "temple" is He really talking about? (v21)

▶ What event, which happened over "three days", do you think Jesus is talking about?

We don't worship God today by going to a place, but to a person. In the Lord Jesus, we can meet and know the mighty God of Psalm 99. The way we exalt God in our lives is by treating the crucified, risen Jesus as King over our lives.

▶ In which area of your life could you live with Jesus as King more today?

76 – REPEAT REPEAT REPEAT REP...

▶ What picture does the psalmist paint at the end of verse 3?

Read John 10 v 14–30

▶ Who is the shepherd of God's sheep? (v14)

▶ Pick out all the amazing things that He does for His sheep.

▶ Why is it wonderful to know that as Christians we are "the sheep of his pasture"?

77 – I WILL (WILL I?)

Read 2 Samuel 11 and pick out the ways David broke his promises of Psalm 101.

▶ *How did God react? (v27)*

Read Mark 1 v 9–11

▶ *How did God react to the life of Jesus?*

God the Father was always well pleased with the thoughts, words and actions of His Son, Jesus. Imagine that — a man who never, ever displeased the all-seeing, perfect God! And then pause to appreciate the fact He died on the cross and experienced God's displeasure at all the wrong David, you and me have ever done. And then take some time simply to thank Him for doing that. It's amazing!

78 – TROUBLING TIMES

Re-read verses 25–27

These words are written by the psalmist about God. But he's being guided in every word by God Himself. And the mind-bending thing is that actually God says these words to someone else…

Read Hebrews 1 v 8–12

▶ *Look back at verse 8. Who is God speaking to? (v8)*

▶ *What are verses 10–12 telling us about God's Son, Jesus?*

▶ *How do these verses make it even more amazing that Jesus came to earth as a human?*

▶ *How do they make it even more exciting that we can know Him as our brother?*

▶ *Why will it help to remember these things when we're struggling in life?*

MATTHEW

79 – FOLLOW THE LEADER

Read verse 27

▶ *What does it mean to know God?*

▶ *How thankful are you for that relationship?*

▶ *What's the only way to come to know God?*

Read verse 28

"Rest" doesn't mean an easy life, but it's relief from human religion, a rest from trying to be good enough for God with the prospect of being part of God's future rest (Hebrews 4 v 1–11).

80 – SABBATH SCANDAL

Verses 1–14 aren't about Sundays or rules. They're about Jesus. As God's promised King, He came to complete what was in the Old Testament. So serving God now means following Jesus. Something those Pharisees weren't prepared to do.

Read verse 8 again

When Jesus says He's Lord of the Sabbath, He means more than just that He decides what could happen on the Jewish day of rest. It also means He's in charge of heaven, where God Christians will ultimately fully enjoy God's rest. That's a double shock for the Pharisees — Jesus says He's God, the one in charge of the

Sabbath. But He's also saying: "If you want to get to heaven and know God's forgiveness, you need to come to me".

Read Matthew 12 v 15–21
and thank God for:
• who Jesus is (v18)
• what He is like (v19-20)
• what He did (v20)
• and what He will do (v21)

81 – DEVIL'S ADVOCATE

Read Titus 3 v 5 for more about Jesus' forgiveness and the work of the Holy Spirit. Why not learn this verse by heart?

82 – SOMETHING FISHY

Just as in the days of the prophet Jonah, it would be outsiders (Gentiles) who'd turn to God. That would be the sign. But Jesus said these Pharisees had enough evidence already (v41–42). If outsiders like the Nineveh guys (in Jonah's time) or the Queen of Sheba (in Solomon's time) had listened to God's messengers, how much more responsible were these guys who had Jesus in front of their eyes?

Read the parable of the tenants in the vineyard in Matthew 21 v 33–46.
ⓓ *What do the evil tenants recognise? (v38)*
ⓓ *What do they do? (v39)*
ⓓ *Who are the tenants supposed to represent? (v45)*
ⓓ *Does this surprise you?*

83 – HIDE AND SEED

We think we've got Jesus sorted and then — WHAM! — He's shocked us again. He's saying that He spoke in parables to hide the truth, not reveal it. God's truth isn't gained by natural insight. And God chooses who He reveals it to. Those serious about following Jesus, those who asked Him questions (like the disciples, v10), were given an explanation. Those who weren't, who didn't, were left in the dark.

Read 1 Corinthians 1 v 18–31
ⓓ *How does the non-Christian world assess what God is doing? (v18, v21–23)*
ⓓ *How does God show His wisdom and power? (v23–25)*
ⓓ *Can we depend on or boast in our own abilities or intellect? (v27–31)*

84 – SEEDS REVEALED

Jesus wants His hearers (that's us!) to seek His help to be good soil, each time we hear Him. So how are you doing?

Read verses 20–22
ⓓ *Are your roots deep?*
ⓓ *Are you firmly rooted in Christ or will trouble and persecution cause you to fade away?*
ⓓ *Are worries and possessions choking your love for Jesus?*
ⓓ *Do you need to do some weeding in your life?*

85 – WEED IT AND REAP

How does this parable help you to answer the following questions:

▷ *Why are so many people opposed to God?*
▷ *Why do the wicked seem to prosper?*
▷ *Will God ever punish them?*

Use your answers to fuel your prayers for yourself, the church in your country and Christians around the world who suffer for following Christ.

86 – CUTTING THE MUSTARD

How will what you have learned about the power and influence of God's King and kingdom (despite their humble appearances) help you today as you try to stand firm as a Christian in the classroom, on the bus, round the meal table?

87 – TRUE TREASURE

Look back over all the parables Jesus has told in chapter 13. Make a note of what you have learned about the kingdom of heaven (life with Jesus) from each one.

-
-
-
-
-
-
-

88 – ROOTS OF REJECTION

This idea of a spiritual family comes up again and again in the Bible. Check out the following verses:

Psalm 27 v 10
Mark 10 v 28–31
Acts 28 v 14–15

▷ *How do you need to change your view of your Christian family?*

89 – MURDER IN MIND

Remember what Jesus told His disciples to expect? **Read Matthew 10 v 17–31** and see how what happened to John the Baptist was not so surprising.

▷ *Are you prepared to follow Jesus knowing what it might mean?*

90 – BREAD ROLE

Jesus' miracles are often signposts pointing to a truth about Jesus and His kingdom. Read the parallel account of this event in **John 6 v 25–58** and work out what Jesus is revealing about Himself, His kingdom and His mission.

91 – FOCUS ON JESUS

Read verses 28–31 again

A rush of blood to Peter's brain... but the lesson's clear: trust isn't sitting back hoping things will work out, but it's an active, ongoing reliance on God's promises.

▷ *In what situations do you need to start trusting Him?*

RSVP

engage wants to hear from YOU!

▶ Share experiences of God at work in your life
▶ Any questions you have about the Bible or the Christian life?
▶ How can we make *engage* better?

Email us — **martin@thegoodbook.co.uk**

Or send us a letter/postcard/cartoon/treasure chest to:

engage 37 Elm Road, New Malden, Surrey, KT3 3HB, UK

In the next **engage**

2 Kings Crumbling kingdom
Matthew Controversial Jesus
2 Corinthians Power in
weakness
Jude Fight for the faith
Plus: Spiritual enemies
Can we trust the Bible?
Non-Christian family
Bible translations

Order **engage** now!

Make sure you order the next issue of **engage**. Or even better, grab a one-year subscription to make sure **engage** lands in your hands as soon as it's out.

Call us to order in the UK on `0333 123 0880`
International: `+44 (0) 20 8942 0880`

or visit your friendly neighbourhood website:
UK: www.thegoodbook.co.uk
N America: www.thegoodbook.com
Australia: www.thegoodbook.com.au
New Zealand: www.thegoodbook.co.nz

Growing
with God

Faithful, contemporary Bible reading resources for every age and stage.